Request for information should be addressed to:

ONE Extraordinary Marriage, 12550 Senda Panacea, San Diego, CA 92129

Or email: info@oneextraordinarymarriage.com

ISBN: 978-0-578-99145-0

QUICKLY FIND, FOCUS ON AND FIX ANY CRACKS IN YOUR MARRIAGE...

The 6 Pillars of Intimacy quiz will help you see which pillars have cracks so you can focus on what your marriage needs most - right now.

Take Your FREE Quiz Today!

This quiz is delivered completly online!

Welcome to The 6 Pillars of Intimacy Quiz

This quiz will help you see which of the pillars are causing the cracks so you can focus on what your marriage needs most.

CLICK HERE TO START

It's easy to complete and in just minutes, you'll have the answers your marriage needs most.

Get Started Now

Readers who download and use The 6 Pillars of Intimacy quiz, in conjunction with this book, are able to implement the strategies faster and take the next steps to create an extraordinary marriage.

You can get your FREE quiz by visiting:
www.OneExtraordinaryMarriage.com/quiz

DEDICATION

To every person who is courageous and does what it takes to make their marriage extraordinary, your commitment is an inspiration to us.

Love you guys!

CONTENTS

A QUICK NOTE

THE VOICES IN THIS BOOK

The 6 Pillars of Intimacy was written by Alisa, so all references to I, me, my, mine are Alisa speaking. Tony shares his insights in key areas, and we designate those with "Tony's Thoughts."

USING HUSBAND AND WIFE

Throughout this book, you will see that we use the terms "husband" and "wife," "him" and "her," and "spouses." On October 5, 1996, our wedding officiant declared us husband and wife. Spouses. This is our identity. Throughout our entire marriage, and since we began talking to couples and studying marriage in 2010, these are the words we have used.

We understand different couples use different words. We invite you to substitute whatever words work for you, and we appreciate you allowing us to use what is meaningful to us. One of the key aspects of a successful marriage is the ability to pursue understanding, even when the two of you aren't using the same words. The same is true of us having a successful relationship with you. We might not use the same words, but the principles surrounding the 6 Pillars of Intimacy will bear themselves out no matter what words you use.

WHY "ONE EXTRAORDINARY MARRIAGE"

The name ONE Extraordinary Marriage was the result of these two ideas:

1. Genesis 2:24: "For this reason a man shall leave his father and his mother, and be united to his wife, and they will become **one** flesh" [emphasis added] has guided us from the beginning of our own marriage transformation. Every day we are on a mission to help couples become one.

2. Our mission has always been to help **one** marriage. We figured if we could make one marriage extraordinary, it could change the world. We have been blessed to impact thousands upon thousands of marriages around the world. Each of these changed marriages leaves a lasting legacy. Yet, we know that we are not done. We get up every day with the mission to impact the one marriage that needs help that day.

WHO IS THE ONE FAMILY

When we speak about the ONE Family, we are referring to the community of podcast listeners, readers, and Facebook and Instagram followers who allow us the privilege of being a part of their marriage story. We use the term family because of what it implies. Families do life together, families weather storms together, families look for a way to make it through. Families are imperfectly perfect.

INTRODUCTION

Write down the revelation and make it plain on tablets so that a herald may run with it. For the revelation awaits an appointed time; it speaks of the end and will not prove false. Though it linger, wait for it; it will certainly come and will not delay.

———

Habakkuk 2:2-3

I s it really possible to rekindle the spark and restore the "like-new" connection in your marriage?

Can you strengthen your bond, evolve and grow together, and enjoy new, deeper levels of love and intimacy that rival your newlywed days?

And, more importantly, can you do any or all of that without having to digest mountains of psychology books or pouring your hearts out in endless counseling sessions?

Yes, it is possible—and as you read, you'll see how easy it can be.

But before we show you, allow us to say hello and introduce ourselves.

We're Tony and Alisa DiLorenzo, and we are passionate about helping couples create their own extraordinary marriage.

Maybe you found your way here through our #1 marriage podcast, "The ONE Extraordinary Marriage Show," through which we connect with an audience of over 50,000 listeners around the world. Or perhaps there was something about the book cover that resonated with where you are in your marriage. Or maybe your spouse just handed you this book and simply said, "Please read this!"

Regardless of how you got here, we're delighted you did! We promise you'll walk away from this book better equipped to have the extraordinary marriage you desire and deserve.

Through reading this book, you're going to discover a totally unique way of understanding your marriage. You'll learn what to do when "cracks" appear, how to repair most of them easily, and how to prevent many cracks from happening in the first place.

Even the best marriages can have cracks in their relationship. The difference is that extraordinary couples take action when they see those cracks happening.

HOW WE DISCOVERED THE CRACKS IN OUR MARRIAGE

When we got married back in 1996, we thought it would be smooth sailing. How hard could marriage be? Happily ever after wasn't just the screen at the end of a movie, it was our expectation. It was probably yours, too.

Boy, were we wrong!

Eleven years later, we were at a crossroads and didn't know which way to go. Our kids were two and five, and parenting was harder than we had ever anticipated. We had clawed our way out of tens of thousands of dollars of debt only to have the Great Recession threaten our financial stability again. We had dealt with Tony's pornography addiction and the broken trust that resulted from that confession. We had amassed a hefty list of marital challenges, and even though we thought we had worked through them, we found ourselves further apart than ever.

A good analogy is that it felt like being in the same grocery store at the same time, but not shopping together or discussing what needs to be purchased. Sure, we were living together, but there was no depth.

We were so dysfunctional that we were face-to-face with the possibility of divorce.

Fortunately, God had different plans for us. One night, we were watching a replay of a morning talk show where our friends' kids had been featured in a beach tennis segment. Right after the kids segment was a story about two couples who had done sex challenges in their marriages. One couple had sex for 101 days straight and in the other marriage, a wife gifted her husband a year of sex for his 40th birthday.

Tony immediately suggested that we could do this as part of the eight-week small group that we would be leading at our church. The study was focused on studying sex, specifically in the Song of Solomon as presented in the book, Intimacy Ignited.[1] If we were going to be talking about sex for eight weeks, why not "practice what we were preaching?" I immediately said "No" because at the time, we weren't spending any time being close to each other, let alone having sex.

> When you are focused on your spouse for a concentrated amount of time, you get more in tune with who they are, their concerns, their joys.

The next day, I had a "come to Jesus" moment when I realized that Tony wasn't asking me to do anything crazy. He was asking me to make our marriage a priority. The hope was that if we were intentional about this, it might help restore some sort of connection to each other.

Wow, did that challenge give us more than we bargained

for! It brought to light the things that had been slowly, consistently, and—in many cases—invisibly eroding the foundation of our marriage. When we made the commitment to have sex every day, it meant that we had to look at *all* aspects of our marriage. We couldn't just go through the motions. Choosing to be sexually intimate every day, choosing that level of vulnerability and connection doesn't just happen. When you are focused on your spouse for a concentrated amount of time, you get more in tune with who they are, their concerns, their joys. It happens through the conversations, through the touches, through the looks that you give one another. You become more aware of what's working and what's not in the marriage. In other words, we discovered the reasons behind our cracks.

It wasn't just the lack of sex that was impacting our marriage—although that was part of it.

Once we started to focus on one another, we realized that we had fallen into living like roommates. We could handle all the logistics of doing life together, but had lost the emotional and physical connection. Everything was about survival. What did we need to do to get through today, to make sure that the kids were okay and the bills were paid. There was nothing else.

This concentrated time highlighted the fact that we'd stopped really hugging or kissing each other—it was more like a quick peck, if it was anything. And at that time, we were so focused on the kids that we'd forgotten what it was like to spend time together, just the two of us. When we were committed to the 60-Day Sex

Challenge, we had to go beyond the surface. We had to break out of our routines. Focusing on our marriage and each other made us realize that we had lost the ability to communicate and even the ability to laugh.

We looked good on the outside, but on the inside, we were a mess!

As the days passed, and we were focused on one another and making our marriage a priority, we could see these cracks and their causes. And we began to address them. The reality was that we had to take action or it was clear that we would end up as a divorce statistic. *Both of us* focused on doing things differently, and—wonder of wonders—our marriage started to improve.

People started to notice and ask what our secret was. As we shared our unusual story of transformation with other couples, word began to spread. Before we knew it, we were being asked to speak to groups and work with other couples.

Over time, we realized there were many common factors that occur in every marriage, but pretty quickly, one thing began to stick out above all else:

THERE ARE SIX INTIMACIES AT THE HEART OF EVERY EXTRAORDINARY MARRIAGE

Since 2010, we've spent countless hours studying not only our marriage, but the marriages of other couples around the world. These six intimacies have shown themselves to us time and time again. Once we noticed this pattern, the observation was so exciting to us, we started sharing it with the world.

We now call these intimacies the six "pillars," because they are the support structures that hold a marriage together.

As long as the pillars are solid and straight, they will keep your marriage thriving and ensure everything goes along smoothly.

The best way to strengthen and help your marriage is to take care of your *6 Pillars of Intimacy*.

But if they lean, form cracks, or become damaged, your marriage will start to collapse.

Research shows that couples go through an average of six years of being unhappy before getting help.[2]

Many folks wait too long and get to the point where they believe it's too late for their marriage. It doesn't have to be that way. We know this, both from personal experience and from seeing the marriages of countless people we have worked with improve.

The best way to strengthen and help your marriage is to take care of your *6 Pillars of Intimacy.*

You might now be thinking, "Well, if that's the key, just tell me what the 6 Pillars are so I can get to work."

Knowledge is one thing, but action is something else altogether. Extraordinary marriages don't "just happen," and they don't come from reading one page of condensed information. They result from being intentional and taking action.

We didn't just snap our fingers or wish for a better marriage. We made the decision to do something different, to invest in our marriage. We realized we knew little about how to do marriage well, and needed to change that about ourselves in order to improve.

We want you to have an extraordinary marriage, and we want you to get to that place much faster than we did. It's your turn to get started on that road to extraordinary... now.

We know how hard it can be when things are wrong in your marriage, but we also know how *incredible* it feels when things turn around. You deserve to have an extraordinary marriage. The 6 Pillars of Intimacy will show you the way. It's time for you to have your breakthrough!

CHAPTER 1

WHAT NO ONE EVER TOLD YOU
ABOUT MARRIAGE

A wedding is an event, a marriage is a lifetime. Invest more in your marriage than your wedding and success is inevitable.

Anonymous

Once upon a time, a handsome guy saw a beautiful woman. They struck up a conversation, one conversation led to another, and they soon found themselves on a first date. They had so much fun that they had a second date, and a third, and a fourth.

As they got to know each other, they realized they were falling in love. Some time passed, then he asked her the question: "Will you marry me?"

It did not surprise their friends and family when she said, "Yes!"

They planned the wedding, which went off without a hitch. It was easier than they expected to plan the wedding. There were so many sites and books and resources to help them find all the "right" things to make those six hours magical. Suddenly, they were husband and wife.

After the honeymoon, it was fun to set up their first place together, to dream about what their lives would look like, what their kids would be like. But after a while, they started to wonder, "Why aren't we getting along so well?" Little things got annoying. Which way does the toilet paper go? How hard is it to get your dirty clothes in the hamper? Were you always so messy? Why is it hard for us to talk, or even just make time to talk?

After the kids came, they found that there was even less time for dates or sex, or even just hanging out. Those little fights about toilet paper and dirty clothes became bigger fights about happiness and not understanding one another, and questioning why they ever thought it was a good idea to get married in the first place.

They knew something was wrong, but they couldn't

quite figure out what it was, or what to do about it. And they were scared that if they didn't figure it out, they were never going to be happy together—or worse, they might not make it.

This was us, for the first eleven years of our marriage. Maybe it sounds a little too familiar to what's going on in your own marriage.

We got married thinking that everything was going to be rainbows and unicorns. We thought we would be the couple that *easily* made it to our sunset years. "Happily ever after" was the goal and the dream, and we expected it would be an easy goal to achieve.

Except, we didn't know how to create "happily ever after." We got married thinking that the marriage would take care of itself. We loved each other, so how hard could being married to the same person for the rest of our lives be?

It turns out that being married is a lot harder—and a lot more challenging—than planning a wedding.

There are lots of reasons why this is true.

CHALLENGE #1: YOUR SPOUSE IS GOING TO HANDLE LIFE DIFFERENTLY

The two of you had different upbringings. You have different views on marriage. You value different things. Your communication styles are not the same. How you show affection is different, and every family has different types of dysfunction.

Regardless of what you see on social media,

everyone's family has some level of dysfunction. When you are dealing with human beings, dysfunction is part of the equation. It's important to figure out what yours is so you can address it, because anything left undealt with will come out under stress in your marriage.

There are all these differences, and yet on your wedding day an officiant declared you "Mr. and Mrs."

A unit.

One.

Except, you are *not* one. You are still two, and it's that two-ness that causes all the challenges in marriage.

We want you to know that it's normal to wish that your spouse was more like you. It's normal to lament the fact that it would be so easy if he/she could just get on board with your way of doing things. But think about this: if your spouse was just like you, one of you wouldn't be necessary.

Marriage is about learning to build a life with another human being. It's a journey in finding unity and loving someone through many different seasons, not only the fun ones.

CHALLENGE #2: MARRIAGE DOESN'T COME WITH A MANUAL

Marriage is one of the few things in life that requires true on-the-job training. It doesn't matter if you feel like he knows you better than anyone ever has, or if she's the one you can say anything to. Once the wedding is over and real life begins, you may find yourself scratching your head and thinking, "Who is this person I've married?"

A good number of you reading this book likely had some sort of premarital counseling or coaching, but did it even skim the surface of what marriage was really going to be like? You read the books and had the conversations, but it was all hypothetical back then. Now, you are in the real world, and none of that training is helping.

How can you learn to resolve fights and talk through your differences when you grew up in a family where your parents never fought in front of you? Or where they fought in front of you, but never seemed to resolve anything? You never got to witness what it looks like for a couple to deal with and work through the day-to-day challenges that come with marriage.

What happens if your parents were never affectionate in front of the kids, so you don't know what that looks like, and now you are married to someone who is begging you to be more affectionate? Your spouse wants you to touch them, but what does that even mean?

> Wherever you are, whatever your story has been, it's okay. You are not alone.

Maybe you saw your parents simply tolerating each other for the sake of the kids. They were excellent (or not-so-excellent) roommates, but nothing more. You may know how to put the kids first, but have no clue how to put your spouse first.

It could be that your parents divorced, and you never got to experience a couple working through their challenges. Because of this, you may not know how to be vulnerable, or how to choose connection when all you want to do is to flee or fight. Maybe you were raised by a single parent and never saw the interaction between husband and wife. Or your single parent dated a lot and you never saw what it looked like for a couple to build a marriage during different seasons.

Wherever you are, whatever your story has been, it's okay. You are not alone. You're starting this book with the idea that you need something more, and you are willing to work to find the solution. Keep reading. You're holding the answers in your hands.

CHALLENGE #3: YOU'LL HAVE TO FIGHT AGAINST COMPARISON

Comparison is real and it will steal your joy when it comes to your marriage. It shows up in so many different ways. It happens when you are looking at someone's Facebook or Instagram posts of a fabulous date or vacation and thinking why can't that be us. Or when you see a couple out on a date and they look like they are having fun while the two of you are struggling to have a conversation. It's seeing a co-worker respond to a sweet or sexy text from their spouse and thinking "I don't ever get texts like that."

It's easy to think that everyone else has a perfect marriage and feel frustrated or defeated when the two of you are struggling. You see the highlight reel, a snapshot in time. This crafted narrative of a perfect marriage is what they *want* you to see, but it is not always reality. Choosing which picture to post is intentional, because they are choosing what story they want to tell through the pictures people see.

CHALLENGE #4: YOU MIGHT FALL INTO BEING ROOMMATES

Couples don't get married and think the passion will disappear, or that, in the future, they won't have much to talk about except the logistics of their lives. No one thinks that, at some point, they'll look at their spouse and think, "You're an incredible parent, but I'm not attracted to you."

No one gets married thinking these things, and yet the result, roommate syndrome, is so common. It might happen after having kids, or when careers change, or when the kids leave for college. Without intentionality in each of your 6 Pillars, roommate syndrome can easily lead into considering an affair or divorce.

When you find yourself in roommate syndrome, it's easy to think that there's someone else out there who can better meet your needs. It's easy to think that it's no big deal if you end your marriage, as you'd both be better for it. It's easy to think it's all your spouse's fault.

Roommate syndrome happens when you aren't intentional about your marriage. It's the result of not investing your time, energy, or resources in this relationship. It's an expectation that everything will be fine, even without effort.

CHALLENGE #5: MARRIAGE DOESN'T LOOK LIKE THE MOVIES

Truth time. How many of you have watched a Hollywood romance and thought, "That's what I want for my marriage," immediately followed by, "Why can't we be like that? Why is marriage so hard for us?"

I'll raise my hand. In the early years of our marriage, I wanted the Hollywood fairy tale. I wanted all our problems to neatly wrap up in two hours, where my hair is always perfect, the lighting is just right, and the script is always just what needs to be said.

> **Most couples don't have 276 people helping them get the love story figured out.**

Our marriage wasn't (and still isn't) like that. It's messy and awkward. Sometimes we don't look our best, and sometimes we say the wrong things.

Oh, and about those perfect, Hollywood, happily-ever-after endings...when the credits roll, you'll see there are, on average, 276 people involved in making that movie happen.[1] It's pretty safe to say that if you had 276 people helping you pick the words to say, fluffing the pillows, cleaning the room, getting your makeup on and your clothes picked out, your marriage would be a lot easier, too.

Most couples don't have 276 people helping them get the love story figured out. You don't have a script or a manual; it's up to the two of you, and that often means you have to do something you never expected to have to do: be *intentional.*

WHY INTENTIONALITY IS THE GAME CHANGER

We are intentional in so many areas of our lives:

- Want to get in shape? Hire a trainer. Get a treadmill. Sign up for classes at the gym.
- Want to improve your financial picture? Start saving. Get a financial advisor. Invest in your retirement plan.
- Want to have an extraordinary marriage? ...*crickets*. How do you do that? Who do you look to for guidance?

Finding the path to an extraordinary marriage can often seem elusive. I hear from so many people who say they didn't think marriage would be this hard. They know they love each other, but struggle with the fact that it was easy before—before kids, before jobs, before the parents got older, before finances got tight, before, before, before.

In the early stages of your relationship, it's assumed that you were highly intentional. You had to make the choice to ask this person out (or to say yes, if you were the one asked). Your outfits were carefully thought out. You thought about what the two of you would do. There was a natural curiosity to get to know the other person, to understand them. There was a desire to do things with them and for them.

Then the proposal came, and all the wedding planning.

The colors.

The cake.
The food.
The dress.
The tuxedo.
Everything was discussed and planned and, well, intentional. Why? Because it all *mattered*.

And then, after saying "I do," time goes by and life gets busy and you both get really comfortable with one another.

> Intentionality is a game changer, because everyone wants to feel important.

Throughout all of that, you stop working so hard on the marriage, on getting to know how your spouse is growing and changing, and that's when the drifting apart starts. This drift is something no one talks about, and it leads you to ask questions like: Am I with the right person? Is this the right relationship for me? Is there something better out there? Would I be happier with someone else? Did I ever love my spouse?

STOP.

You've stopped being intentional. You've been on autopilot, just going through the motions. Your marriage was never supposed to be so-so. People don't get married to have an "OK" life. When you choose to get intentional and to take action in your marriage, you are demonstrating that this relationship is a priority, and that your spouse is a priority.

Intentionality is a game changer, because everyone wants to feel important. Time and time again in marriage coaching, I hear statements like:

- I don't think my spouse knows who I am anymore.
- I just want to feel seen.
- My spouse doesn't hear me.
- I can't remember the last time we spent real time together.
- It feels like we are just roommates.

Maybe you've said these yourself. If you have said these (or even just thought them), I want you to know that it's okay. I get it. As I journey with you through this book, it's going to be like sitting down with a friend, having a cup of coffee. We'll be talking about intimacy in a way that you've likely never heard before, and by the end, you'll be equipped to make your own marriage extraordinary.

This book isn't just a book for you to read passively, or to take up space on the nightstand. This book is your "Aha" moment. Within these pages, you'll see yourself and your marriage. You'll see where you are and where you want to be. Most importantly, you'll see hope for what you want to become.

To get started, let's talk about what intimacy is... and what it isn't.

CHAPTER 2

INTIMACY IS MORE THAN SEX

Vulnerability is not winning or losing. It's having the courage to show up and be seen when we have NO control over the outcome.

Brene Brown

S ome of you just read the title of this chapter and thought, "Yeah, right, Alisa and Tony. What do you mean intimacy is more than just sex?"

If we asked one hundred people, "What's the first thing that you think of when you hear the word 'intimacy'?" there's a high probability that while some might mention emotional intimacy, close to a hundred of them would say something related to sex. We're conditioned to think of "sex" and "intimacy" as interchangeable words.

Except they're not.

When we first got married, we thought these words were the same thing. We didn't know what we didn't know. We figured that if we were having sex, we were in a good place.

Right?

But what happens when you aren't having sex all the time, or even any of the time? Or when you aren't really talking to one another, and you're keeping secrets from one another, and you don't spend time together. What happens when you feel as close as Los Angeles and Paris?

We spent over a decade of our marriage struggling to understand how to be intimate. Yes, we'd do a date night here and there, and we'd go on vacation. From the outside, we looked like we had it all together, maybe, but inside our marriage, it felt like the Sahara Desert. Dry and desolate. Why were we struggling to communicate? What happened to the couple who loved spending time together? I mean, even at our worst, we were still having sex sometimes,

Intimacy in marriage is not just sex.

so why didn't it feel like we had any intimacy in our marriage?

Intimacy in marriage is not just sex. The idea that sex and intimacy are the same thing has been tripping up couples forever. If you really think about it, the idea that sex and intimacy are the same makes little sense. You can't have sex 24/7, but you can have intimacy with your spouse all throughout the day.

Real intimacy is the closeness and connection that can only be created between a husband and wife. You are a multidimensional human being, so why would intimacy be one dimensional? Why would it only be about sex?

So many times we'll get messages from people, just like you, who will say things like:

- I can't figure out why we aren't closer.
- I don't know why we can't seem to get along.
- I just wish I felt more connected to my spouse.

At the heart of each of these statements is the desire for a deeper connection with your spouse that you can't get just anywhere. You don't want the surface relationship. You don't want to be going through the motions. You *want* to see your spouse and be seen by them. You have a desire for connection and closeness that includes sex, but is so much more than that.

WHAT IS INTIMACY, BEYOND SEX?

Sex is only one way couples can be intimate with one another. When "sex" and "intimacy" are used interchangeably, you are ignoring so many other ways to be close and connected to your spouse. You are making your relationship one dimensional, and putting a lot of pressure on your marriage (and each other).

> **Becoming one isn't just about having sex with your spouse—it's about sharing all parts of yourself with them.**

You can also be intimate with your spouse with your emotions and words, with how you touch one another, with your finances, with your spirituality, and with how you choose to spend time with one another. Seeing intimacy in this way changes your view of your marriage and the possibilities within your relationship.

Every day, you have choices to make about the words you speak, about how you'll spend your time and your money, about how you will physically interact with your spouse, about what you'll share with them, etc. These areas cover your entire life.

In Matthew 19:5, we read: "For this reason, a man will leave his father and mother and be united to his wife, and the two will become one flesh."

Becoming one isn't just about having sex with your spouse—it's about sharing all parts of yourself with them. It's a choice to be known by another person. It's a choice to step into a place where you can be loved for who you are—for all aspects of yourself, both the parts you're really proud of and the parts that still need work or still need to be healed. It's also a choice to know who they are in whatever season they are in.

Choosing to be intimate with your spouse is choosing to give them the gift of who you are. It's choosing to grow with another human being. It's not uncommon to have growing pains. Sometimes you have to figure out new ways to do things, and adjust your understanding of where you are once you have reached a new season. Sometimes you outgrow old ways of doing things and have to learn new ways of doing something. That's okay.

When we first got married, we didn't have kids. We could come and go as we liked. We could take off for a weekend. Stay up late and sleep in. We had the ability to do what we wanted, when we wanted. We figured out how to be a dual income couple, even with the challenges of working opposite shifts or working far from home. It was just the two of us and we thought we were normal. We were young and making it work, yes we had struggles in our communication and we fought about sex but doesn't everyone?

Six years later, we had our first child. Suddenly, leaving the house was like a small military operation. He wasn't the best sleeper, and he wouldn't take a bottle. It felt like I was on duty all the time. Gone were the "Hey, let's just take off" weekends and "let's sleep in" mornings. Our old ways of showing our love for one another were no longer possible. We had grown into a new season and a lot of the frustration was because we didn't know how to be intimate, close, and connected when the circumstances had changed.

This is why understanding that intimacy is more than

just sex is so important.

We've now entered another new season where that same baby has left for college. Our home dynamic has shifted, and we are again in a growing season. We are learning how to be intentional in our intimacy all over again.

It doesn't matter what season you are in, in your life or in your marriage. What matters is that you have a desire to learn all that you can about how to be intimate, in every area, with your spouse.

When you choose to give them your entire self, when you choose to grow with them, what the two of you will create will be nothing short of extraordinary. It's setting the two of you up for success.

CHAPTER 3

SET YOURSELF UP FOR SUCCESS

Every success story is a tale of constant adaptation, revision and change.

Richard Branson

Success in marriage doesn't "just happen." It's the result of awareness and intentional action. Awareness of what's happening in your life, in your spouse's life, and in the world around you *and* action that will make a difference to those involved.

I can't tell you how many times we were dealing with a situation in our marriage when this thought flashed through my head: "If only Tony would…" So many times I have wanted him to take action first. Other times, I was acting out of stubbornness or fear or even just the expectation that it was his responsibility to fix us or change what he was doing, so that I could be more loving/kinder/nicer. You name it, I've thought of it.

I wasted so much time on all the things I thought *he* needed to do. There was only one problem.

He wasn't the *only* one who needed to take action in our marriage.

When I was waiting for Tony to change, or take action, or go first, I wasn't working on the most important person I could change: ME.

Like a lot of individuals, I didn't want to have to confront the person in the mirror and say to her, "What can I do to change how we are connecting right now?"

Until I was willing to look at the woman in the mirror and get real with what I could do, our marriage had reached the ceiling. As Michael Jackson sang in the song "Man in the Mirror,"

I'm starting with the man in the mirror. I'm asking him to change his ways.[1]

WHAT CAN I DO?

Change starts with you. You have to change before your spouse can or will. When you adopt a "What Can I Do?" mindset in your marriage, you can take action to shift any area of your relationship.

When you ask "what can I do?", a few things happen:

- You don't focus on what your spouse needs to change.
- You aren't telling them what they need to do.
- You aren't complaining about what's happening.
- You aren't putting all the relationship responsibility on them.

When both individuals in a marriage take personal responsibility, the entire dynamic in your relationship changes.

You are stepping up and stepping into the role of leader in your marriage. You are looking at the relationship from a brand new focus.

Try taking responsibility in the following scenarios:

- When you feel like complaining, blaming, or nagging, ask yourself the question, what can I do?
- When things aren't going how you want them to go in the relationship, ask yourself the question, what can I do?
- When you think about planning a date night, a weekend away or the family vacation, ask yourself, what can I do?
- When you are evaluating your sex life, ask yourself, what can I do?

- When you are looking at your finances, ask yourself, what can I do?
- When you are evaluating your spiritual intimacy, ask yourself, what can I do?

If you find yourself in a situation where you are the only one in the marriage who is asking this question, it's time to find a marriage coach. There can be a number of reasons why your spouse is not asking the question or engaging in personal responsibility. Getting help to understand the root cause of this will be a life-changer for you and your marriage. Change starts with you, but it takes two to completely transform a marriage.

WHAT CAN WE DO?

Yes, you start with you—but marriage takes two. Marriage is the ultimate team sport. The best marriages are teams of two people who have different strengths, who see the world differently, who can bring up fresh ideas, and who can take responsibility for different aspects of an issue.

> Marriage is not supposed to be a tug-of-war, with each of you trying to pull the other into the mud.

Your spouse is not supposed to be just like you. They think differently and act differently. They are different. This is a good thing. If the two of you were identical, one of you wouldn't be necessary. This also means that you have to learn to work together in order to be able to answer the question "What can we do?"

So many of my coaching clients have started coaching as opponents instead of teammates. Marriage is not supposed to be a tug-of-war, with each of you trying to pull the other into the mud. Rather, marriage is most successful when the two of you link arms, get on the same side, and face problems together.

When you do this you are looking at each situation and saying, "What can we do?" This mindset recognizes there's a problem that needs to be addressed and solved. It means that the two of you can:

- Strategize solutions.
- Look for win-win outcomes.
- Play to your individual strengths.

You started your marriage walking side-by-side down the aisle, hand-in-hand, unified, ready to tackle the world together. When you say "What can we do?", you bring that mindset into the present. Each one of the chapters covering the 6 Pillars of Intimacy will have both "What Can I Do?" and "What Can We Do?" suggestions to help you take action in your marriage. As you take action, it's important to avoid the common pitfalls.

AVOID THE COMMON PITFALLS

It's not enough to use "What can I do" or "What can we do?" to be successful. You also need to be aware of the most common pitfalls to success: unvoiced expectations, blame, and ultimatums. It's not uncommon for these to show up in a marriage when there are cracks in any of the 6 Pillars of Intimacy. It's important to be aware of them so that you can take action to stop them when they happen.

PITFALL #1: UNVOICED EXPECTATIONS

Everyone has expectations, sometimes you voice them, sometimes you don't. This is especially true in marriage. It's those unvoiced expectations that lead you down a path where you'll say things like:

- If you really loved me, I wouldn't have to tell you.
- We've been together this long, you should know what I like, want, expect.
- I can't believe you don't know that about me.

These statements do nothing to build a connection between the two of you. In fact, it's likely that making statements like this will actually drive the two of you further apart. Make a commitment to voice your expectations, calmly, to your spouse. In all my years of coaching couples, I've found that it's so much easier for one spouse to work together with the other and to actually meet expectations when they know what the expectations are.

> Expressing yourself clearly allows your spouse to be able to take action and meet your needs.

Your spouse cannot read your mind. If your spouse has a moment where it seems like they are reading your mind, don't expect it to happen every single time. The two of you are growing, changing human beings. What you want or like can vary from day to day and hour to hour. Please stop expecting your spouse to read your mind or know exactly what you want. You are making life more difficult for them and for yourself. It's not fair to either of you, and it simply results in frustration, irritation, and resentment. Expressing yourself clearly allows your spouse to be able to take action and meet your needs.

PITFALL #2: BLAME

It's easy to blame your spouse when there are challenges in the marriage. It's human nature. When it's *your* fault, then *I* can be the victim, and *I* don't have any responsibility for what has happened. If it's *your* fault, then it's up to *you* to change things.

The hard part is recognizing the part you, yourself, played in it all. As said in Matthew 7:3-5, *"Why do you look at the speck of sawdust in your brother's eye and pay no attention to the plank in your own eye? How can you say to your brother, 'Let me take the speck out of your eye,' when all the time there is a plank in your own eye? You hypocrite, first take the plank out of your own eye, and then you will see clearly to remove the speck from your brother's eye."*

This passage sums up blame in marriage so well. It's easier to focus on what your spouse has done or needs to do because then the pressure is off of you. When you do this, you lose sight of the fact that how *you* have shown up in the marriage also has had an impact.

Some of you have just thought, "Alisa and Tony, you don't know what my spouse did. They had an affair. They stopped communicating with me. They have withheld sex. This is why I'm blaming them."

It doesn't matter what has happened in the past; it takes two to create every dynamic. It doesn't matter what challenge the two of you are facing in your marriage. There will always be something that *you* can do. In order to strengthen each of the 6 Pillars of Intimacy, you have a role in changing the situation.

Blaming your spouse doesn't make the situation better, and it rarely gets the result you want. Blame often leads to inaction or resistance. Looking in the mirror gets results.

PITFALL #3: ULTIMATUMS

Ultimatums make the relationship conditional, instead of collaborative, creating a "parent/child" or "boss/employee" relationship instead of an equal partnership. "When you X, I'll Y" means that you are making your behavior, or how you show up, conditional on the behavior of your spouse. And that's simply not true.

You are an adult.

You can choose how you show up in the marriage.

You can choose your behaviors.

You can choose your responses.

Your marriage is not about conditions being met; it's about each of you choosing to show up in the relationship, giving 100% to build your extraordinary marriage. Now that you are equipped with the questions that set you up for success and an awareness of the common pitfalls, let's jump into the 6 Pillars of Intimacy.

CHAPTER 4

THE 6 PILLARS OF INTIMACY

Investing in yourself is the best investment you will ever make. It will not only improve your life, it will improve the lives of all those around you.

———

Robin Sharma

B efore we identify the 6 Pillars of Intimacy, it's important to understand why we refer to them as "pillars." Pillars are an architectural design feature used intentionally. Remember when we talked about intentionality before? Looks like our choice for the 'pillar' metaphor was pretty 'intentional' too.

Pillars have very specific features that make them perfect for buildings and for your marriage. They:

- Provide strength
- Add beauty
- Carry weight

What's true in a pillar for a building is true in the pillars of your marriage. When you have strong pillars, your marriage has added strength and beauty and you are able to carry the weight of different seasons of marriage.

When we got married, we didn't know what it would take to have a strong marriage or what extraordinary couples did to be so extraordinary. Yes, we knew that we were supposed to talk to one another and yes, it was important to go on dates. But outside of that we really were just winging it. Our marriage was not beautiful, it wasn't strong, and we definitely didn't have the ability to carry the weight of life.

I think of all the times we didn't have a clue and started to disconnect under the weight of life's circumstances:

- Living paycheck to paycheck, fighting about money, and dodging calls from creditors.
- Tony revealing his pornography addiction.
- Our son, Andrew, dying at 18 weeks gestation.
- Being so busy that there wasn't time for one another.

The list could go on and on. We thought it was normal for a marriage to feel shaky after a couple of years. We figured everyone else was just "grinning and bearing it" because no one was really talking about all the hard stuff. We assumed that marriage wasn't supposed to be good after the honeymoon phase.

We were wrong. On all counts. And like we shared at the beginning, this revelation came when we did the 60-Day Sex Challenge. It came when we realized that the secret to an extraordinary marriage wasn't just good conversations, date nights, and sex.

The secret to an extraordinary marriage *is* the 6 Pillars of Intimacy.

THE 6 PILLARS OF INTIMACY

So, what are the 6 Pillars of Intimacy? We're glad you asked. You've probably already identified a couple of them, but let's introduce all six here:

- Emotional Intimacy
- Physical Intimacy
- Financial Intimacy
- Spiritual Intimacy
- Recreational Intimacy
- Sexual Intimacy

Each of these pillars, like in architecture, provides strength to your marriage, adds beauty to how the two of you interact with each other and the world, and carries weight when you are in different seasons.

You need all six, not just the ones that are easy for

you. Not just the ones that will make your spouse happy. You need ALL. SIX. OF. THEM.

As you learn about each of the six, you'll come to realize a few things about your marriage. For instance, you will now have a name for both connection and disconnection in your marriage. No more trying to grasp at straws about what is going on between the two of you. You may notice that you and your spouse naturally gravitate to one pillar or another, and there will be times when different pillars are stronger or weaker than others.

> The beauty of the pillars is that they become a framework to address any area of your marriage.

By being able to identify the pillar you are having challenges with, you can then seek training or education to strengthen that pillar.

The beauty of the pillars is that they become a framework to address any area of your marriage. Instead of just trying to wing it after you say your vows, you can get focused on these pillars with the purpose of creating your own extraordinary marriage.

Another feature of the pillars is that when you understand what they are and how they operate in your marriage, you can become quicker at identifying when you have cracks in a pillar. A "crack" in a pillar shows up in real life as some form of tension or disconnect. Couples that don't know or understand the 6 Pillars of Intimacy may say things like:

- We'll never be able to fix this.

- We're just so different.
- I can't put my finger on why we just don't seem to get along.

Often, these statements, and the emotions that accompany them (discontent, resentment, bitterness, and sadness, among others), will leave couples wanting to end their marriage, hoping it'll be better with someone else. But you don't have to break up or settle when you can learn to level up your marriage. You don't have to end something that can be fixed.

With the knowledge of the 6 Pillars, couples can develop a vocabulary to talk about what is happening in their marriage without blame or hostility, but rather with genuine concern and a desire to build the marriage stronger.

Most people come into marriage with no idea how to make it to the "happily ever after" phase. When you have a framework and can identify where you are strong and where you need to get stronger, you no longer just have a dream of a good marriage—you can create a plan to get there.

So many marriage resources talk about what *he* needs to do or what *she* needs to do in order for the marriage to be happy or fulfilling. The 6 Pillars of Intimacy is about equipping the two of you to work together, instead of pushing against each other.

On the day that you spoke your wedding vows, the two of you joined the same team. No matter what has happened in your marriage, no matter what has tried to pull the two of you apart, you are on the same team. The

6 Pillars of Intimacy is your game plan, the tool you'll use over and over again to strengthen your communication, bring more laughter to your marriage, have fun together, work through tough seasons, and be there for each other to ultimately create a marriage you *want* to be in. You are different, yet you both want the same thing: to create an extraordinary marriage.

A WORD ABOUT HUSBANDS AND WIVES

Before we tackle the 6 Pillars of Intimacy individually, we need to address the fact that husbands and wives are different.

Husbands, you cannot expect your wife to be just like you. Wives, you cannot expect your husband to be just like you. Trying to make your spouse just like yourself is virtually impossible and places an unfair burden on them. There are women who struggle to connect emotionally with their husband, women who don't talk as much as TV shows and popular culture would have you believe. There are also men who are very strong in their emotional intimacy. Men for whom discussing their feelings or "using their words" is easy. Some women have a high desire for sex, and some men do not. Some men don't really care that much for physical touch, and some women care a lot. Some women are really interested in finances, and some men not so much.

No pillar is always stronger in men or always stronger in women. The intimacies are not male or female. The 6 Pillars of Intimacy is the framework to help the two of you deepen the closeness and connection in your marriage.

Allow yourself to put the stereotypes aside and consider how you and your spouse, personally, can strengthen your marriage by strengthening these pillars.

Give yourself permission to look at the 6 Pillars of Intimacy as a framework that allows both of you to grow into being an extraordinary spouse who is part of a team that is creating an extraordinary marriage. Read this book with the expectation of what's possible.

Take this testimonial from one of my coaching clients:

Today is our 31st wedding anniversary and day 47 in a row of sexual intimacy, and I can honestly say I've never been more in love with my husband. Due to what we have learned, the last 47 days have been the most wonderful we have ever had in our whole marriage.

I had a complete mind shift and was suddenly not angry at my husband anymore. We have talked more often and more deeply than we ever have before. Everything has changed. Before, we had discussed divorce. I didn't want that, but I also didn't want another 30 years of the same. I just didn't know how to fix it.

I had been to counselors several times, and they just didn't help. My husband didn't like counseling, because it just made him feel defensive. Neither of us had the skills or the role models for a healthy marriage. Somehow, this framework reached us and gave us the ability to open up to each other and communicate like we never have. Without anger and hurt, we can share and discuss all our issues.

My husband used to ask me, "Why isn't 'good enough' good enough?"

He later admitted he didn't know how bad it was until he knew how good it could be. This is what I always wanted and dreamed our marriage would be, and now it's come true! We will never go back to the way it was.

I had a coworker recently tell me they want to be like us when they have been together as long as we have. What a compliment!

— L. S. (wife)

This isn't some made-up couple. This is a husband and wife, just like you—a couple willing to try something new, to step out of their routines, even after over three decades of marriage. This is a couple who got intentional and took action.

And it all started with a conversation because, as you'll see in the next chapter, emotional intimacy is key.

CHAPTER 5

PILLAR #1: EMOTIONAL INTIMACY

Be brave enough to start a conversation that matters.

———

Anonymous

E motional. Intimacy.

Those words have put a smile on the face of some of you, and others just cringed.

Some of you cannot wait to have more emotional connection with your spouse. These two words together... it's like Christmas. Emotions and intimacy? Let's do this!

Others are thinking, "I don't know if I can do this. I don't know if I can share my thoughts and feelings. Emotions are not something I'm comfortable with. That's not who I am. I am not a great communicator."

> Emotional intimacy is the workhorse of the pillars.

Stop.

Breathe.

Emotional intimacy can be learned and shared with your spouse. It's not something only a select few are born with.

First, let's define what "emotional intimacy" is. Emotional intimacy is the closeness and connection that is created through sharing each other's feelings, thoughts, and desires. This includes both verbal and non-verbal communication.

It's more than just, "Can we talk?" Although talking *is* part of it.

Emotional intimacy is the workhorse of the pillars. How you communicate to your spouse, both verbally and non-verbally, impacts every area of your marriage. Emotional intimacy underlies all the other five pillars.

There is an innate desire in all of us to be known, seen,

and valued, but most people are never taught how to have hard conversations in marriage. Maybe you took a communication course in college, read a few books, or even listened to a couple of podcasts, but all of that theory means nothing when you are facing a spouse who doesn't communicate the same way you do.

If you had told us when we first met that this pillar would be a challenge for us, we probably would have laughed. We fell in love talking about anything and everything. We spent hours driving around Colorado, talking about our families, our dreams, our lives—you name it. When we were in a long-distance relationship for a year, we would spend hours every day talking to one another over the phone. Sharing our thoughts and feelings? No problem!

Fast forward a couple years: we're married, have all kinds of responsibilities, and can't remember the last time we actually had a real conversation. We'd go on date night and just sit and eat our food, no actual conversation. If we did talk, it was about paying the bills or the plans the kids had for the weekend.

Sometimes we'd have an "intense discussion," aka a fight/disagreement/difference of opinion, which put our different communication styles front and center. A normal discussion would escalate into an intense one easily, as each of us wanted to make our point and feel heard. It wasn't uncommon for me to shut down like a California blackout if we started fighting. No emotion, no words, just arms crossed and closed off.

Does that sound like you or your spouse?

My withdrawal would lead Tony to become more animated, pressing me to share more, which made me want to flee. All he wanted to do was to work it out and get a resolution, worried that if we dropped the topic, we'd never pick it back up again.

Stubbornness would win out and we'd drop it, because we didn't know how to resolve our differences. We didn't know how to create intimacy with one another. We didn't know how to make it safe. Our marriage was failing in an area which had seemed so strong when we were first dating.

Creating emotional intimacy with another human being isn't something that's typically taught. You will not find a college class on this. You're going to learn from trial and error, like:

- If I say this, how does he respond?
- When she's upset, what is she likely to do?
- Have I made this a place where it's okay to be vulnerable or are we just going through the motions?

In order to have a strong Emotional Intimacy Pillar, you need to know why emotional intimacy is so important.

WHAT YOU SAY AND HOW YOU SAY IT IMPACTS YOUR MARRIAGE

Every word that you speak begins as a thought in your head, which means that no matter if it is a negative or positive word, you are the first person impacted. This means that even if you don't speak the words you are still being impacted by them, and there's a good chance your body language is showing what you are thinking.

Once spoken, they impact you a second time as you hear them. Next, they impact the person that they are spoken to *and* they impact people that are around you or who hear them. This means that what you say to your spouse and how you say it matters.

The words you speak have power.

The words you speak have power. They aren't harmless. No matter what they are, they impact many people even if directed to one.

Do you remember this saying from when you were growing up? *"Sticks and stones may break my bones but words will never hurt me?"* It's not true. Not one bit of it.

Some of the biggest damage that gets inflicted in a marriage comes as the result of the words that are spoken. Stop and think about that for a moment. When you recognize the impact that your words are having on yourself and on your spouse you become empowered to choose something different.

When you find yourself in this place where you are speaking words that aren't having the desired impact in your marriage, it's time to change the words that you speak. There is always some emotion behind the spoken thoughts. Words are not just words. They can convey love, hurt, rejection, compassion, frustration, and so much more.

When you identify the emotion(s) behind the words,

it allows you to get to the heart of the matter. It also allows you to express things fully. By simply changing the words, you are able to get rid of blanket statements. It lets you get specific about your feelings that go beyond angry, mad, or sad. It also identifies what the cause is, which gives the two of you a focus on what can be changed.

WHO, WHAT, WHEN, WHY, WHERE, AND HOW

Every chapter discussing the 6 Pillars of Intimacy will have this section so you can understand how to strengthen that specific pillar.

WHO?

This one should be obvious, but it takes two to have emotional intimacy. One (or both) of you keeping your thoughts to yourself and hoping/wishing/praying that the other person will know what you are thinking or feeling will not work. The two of you both need to be participants.

This also means that things between the two of you should stay between the two of you. It can be a slippery slope when you start sharing an emotional connection with someone of the opposite sex who is not your spouse. Husbands, have your buddies. Wives, connect with your girlfriends. Just don't start turning toward another man or woman to meet your emotional needs.

WHAT?

What should you communicate with your partner? The quick answer is "everything." An extraordinary marriage isn't just about discussing the logistics of your life. Extraordinary couples connect on the little things and the not so little things. Your marriage needs conversations around what your schedule looks like *and* how much you love each other. Your marriage will thrive when it's a safe place to talk about your fears and worries as well as your dreams and successes. Learning to share around all of the areas of your life is key because if it's impacting you, it's impacting your spouse and your marriage. A marriage does not do well when you are unable to be vulnerable and share with your spouse. Developing the ability to share *all* aspects of your life can be accomplished, and your world will be a lot better when it is.

WHEN?

Timing is key in marriage. When it comes to building your Emotional Intimacy Pillar, you need to think of all of the different times when you can connect. You might know that morning is the best time for the two of you to have quiet time to connect, or after the kids go to bed. It might be that whenever your spouse pops into your head throughout the day, you'll send a text or make a quick call. It could be that the drive home is the perfect time for the two of you to catch up. The most important thing is to develop a rhythm that works for the two of you.

Now, when it comes to the timing of bigger or weightier conversations, you might need to have a little more thought around this "when" question. It can be hard to hear, "Let's talk" at ten o'clock at night or when you are running out the door late for work. Trying to connect when you are hungry or tired or right after work can place undue stress on your marriage. For conversations that might be more emotional, set a time when the two of you can be alert and fully engaged. You may even decide to have a regular time weekly to discuss what's going on in the marriage.

Quick note: Ephesians 4: 26-27 tells us, "In your anger do not sin" (4:26-27). Do not let the sun go down while you are still angry, and do not give the devil a foothold."

Ideally, you would never go to bed angry. However, if the two of you find yourselves late at night in a conversation that seems to be going in circles, it might be because you are exhausted and cannot think clearly. If one of you realizes this, call a timeout so you can get some sleep and schedule time to revisit it the next day. Just make sure to honor this with your spouse; when you honor this commitment, it builds trust.

WHY?

As long as you are alive, you will be growing and changing. This means that the things that matter to you, the things that worry you, the things that excite you are also constantly changing. In order to know who your spouse is now, you need to stay in an emotional connection with them. Your marriage ought to be the safest place on earth for your spouse to grow and share their growth with you.

It's also important to realize that this time that you choose to connect with your spouse builds your marriage.

If you find that either of you are too busy to emotionally connect with one another, over time the lack of time will pull the two of you apart.

WHERE?

This one is so much fun for us to answer. For decades, it seemed like the most common answer to this question was "sitting at the table, across from each other, staring into one another's eyes."

Um, no. That doesn't always work. You *can* have meaningful conversations at the kitchen table, but you can also have them in your car, walking around the neighborhood, sitting at the park, even in your bedroom.

One thing about where you choose to have your conversations—if a particular location has been emotionally charged in the past, we encourage you to try a different location. For example, if you have tried to talk about your sex life in your bed/bedroom at night and it hasn't gone so well, next time, try bringing the topic up on a walk. Or if you always discuss your financial intimacy in your home office or at the kitchen table, trying sitting on the couch in the family room. Maybe you've found yourselves discussing parenting in the kitchen or sitting on the couch, this might be a good one to take the bedroom and away from the kids. There is no rule that says all conversations have to happen in the same place regardless of topic.

HOW?

The million-dollar question: how do you build emotional intimacy? It starts with making a decision on this pillar. It doesn't matter where your emotional intimacy *has been*, where are you willing to take it? In an earlier chapter we talked about "What Can I Do?" You *can be* emotionally intimate with your spouse.

First, consider the fact that emotional intimacy is multifaceted. It is all of your verbal and non-verbal communication. It's not just what you are saying; it's your tone of voice, and what your body is communicating as well.

Your words have power. The words that you choose to communicate to your spouse will stick with them well beyond the conversation. *How* you say the words you chose is also significant. So many of my coaching clients talk about their spouse's tone of voice. The next time the two of you are in a conversation, stop and think, "How do I sound right now?" If your tone of voice is not inviting to your spouse, pause, regroup, and try again. Finally, after observing your tone of voice, look at your body language. Is your body expressing that your spouse and their point of view are important to you, or not so much? Does it show that you are interested, or bored? Are you expressing love, or disgust?

These all contribute to a strong Emotional Intimacy Pillar.

A COMMON CHALLENGE:

"I'm not a talker. I don't like to share my feelings. My spouse wants to talk everything out."

Often in marriage, there is one person who likes to talk more than the other. This is normal, but it can be challenging. Some people are verbal processors—they process information by talking about it. Others are internal processors—they prefer to think things through in their head. One is not better than the other, it's just different.

You don't have to use 10,000 words a day to have strong emotional intimacy in your marriage. You don't have to share every fluctuation in your emotions to have emotional intimacy with your spouse. You can create systems that work for the two of you—systems that are comfortable.

Here's the story of one of my coaching clients:

Married 39 years, they found themselves drifting further and further apart. With the kids out of the house, opposite work schedules, and no language or time to express themselves, it truly felt like they were roommates. The feelings, on both sides of the marriage, had been stuffed down for years. The husband viewed himself as a man of few words. Growing up, he was taught that men didn't express their feelings. The problem was his wife

> **What you are thinking is important to the health of the marriage.**

desperately wanted that emotional connectio
husband. He didn't know how he was going tu ⌣
this challenge, but he knew that he didn't want to keep
doing what he'd been doing.

As they started to work on their marriage, he made a
decision to learn about emotions and what he was feeling
at any given moment. This is an exercise that I often
suggest to clients. You have to know what you are feeling
before you can share it with your spouse. You have to
understand how those emotions impact you so that you
can understand how they impact your spouse. This couple
chose to get a resource called an emotion wheel. This tool
allowed him to start with a base emotion, like anger, and
follow the wheel to get specific. Instead of just being angry,
he learned what it means to be irritated or insecure. Those
subtleties allowed him to use his words to connect with
his wife in a more meaningful way. His willingness created
an incredible transformation.

You have to have a willingness to be vulnerable and
to share what is happening on the inside of you. Your
thoughts matter to your spouse. What you are thinking is
important to the health of the marriage.

CRACKS IN YOUR EMOTIONAL INTIMACY PILLAR

Perhaps you're not sure if you and your spouse have good
emotional intimacy. Sometimes it's easier to recognize
when you *don't* have emotional intimacy, or, in other
words, when there are cracks in this pillar.

Think about how the two of you communicate:

- In an argument, is it common for one of you to shut down (like a blackout)?
- Or get explosively angry (like a volcano)?
- Is it normal for there to be swearing or cursing at one another?
- Is it common for one of you to walk out on a conversation?
- Do either of you threaten divorce?
- Does someone keep emotions/hurts/disappointments locked up inside until they all come spilling out?
- Does the past keep coming up in discussion?
- Do you avoid certain topics because it "never goes well?"
- Do you or your spouse keep secrets from one another?

You don't have to have *all* of these present in your marriage to have cracks in your emotional intimacy. The presence of *any* of these is an indicator that your Emotional Intimacy Pillar needs to be strengthened.

Awareness is only the first step.

What does it look like with a strengthened pillar? Imagine creating a marriage where:

- You're able to have open, honest, and transparent conversations.
- You feel safe being vulnerable and sharing your thoughts and feelings with your spouse.
- There is conversation that flows smoothly back and forth.

- Your body language conveys that you are interested in and willing to listen to your spouse.
- You can show self-control in your tone of voice and the words that you choose.

Below is a testimony from one of my clients who struggled with emotional intimacy:

If we didn't have you to listen to, we surely wouldn't be together today. We didn't know where to turn or what to do. For years, we struggled with our communication and it seemed like we just kept hitting the same challenges over and over again.

What's made the difference?

Being open and honest with each other. Our communication has turned around a full flip! I used to be terrified to bring up even the smallest thing that bothered me. I would sweat and have anxiety attacks just thinking about bringing something up. Understanding that it was okay to schedule time to talk and that we could take a timeout if it started to feel like it was all too much made it easier for me to be able to stay in a conversation.

Over time, I've developed the ability to come to my husband and calmly discuss what bothers me. We may not find a solution right there, but we'll come back to the conversation a few days later with fresh minds. My husband used to have a hard time circling back to conversations to make sure we were done the next day. He didn't understand that the lack of resolution made me more worried and anxious. Now, he'll come up to me and ask if we need to talk more or if I'm satisfied with our conversation from prior days.

We severely lacked emotional intimacy, but now that we

are building it more and more every day, I feel more confident in our relationship and our marriage.

— S. R. (wife)

BABY STEPS

Throughout this book, you'll hear us refer to "baby steps." In coaching, I explain to my clients that babies aren't born knowing how to run—they first need to learn how to roll over, then how to crawl, then how to stand up, then how to take a step, then how to walk, and *then* how to run. At every one of those points are moments of frustration, moments when it feels like they aren't getting anywhere, moments when you can't see any progress...and yet, every day, the baby is getting stronger, developing more knowledge, trying different things.

This is true for a baby, and it's true for marriage.

In each of these intimacies, you will have baby steps, little actions that you can take to strengthen a particular pillar. Will these baby steps have you crossing the finish line? Not yet. But with consistency and commitment, you will create the most extraordinary marriage.

It takes courage to strengthen your emotional intimacy because it takes vulnerability. You learn vulnerability by *both* being a safe space for your spouse to share *and* working with your spouse to create a safe space where you can share.

Before the two of you can work on this, it's important to be aware of how you communicate.

- Do I want to talk about everything, or talk about very little?
- Am I comfortable bringing anything up to my spouse, or are there certain topics I tend to avoid?
- If so, what are those topics?
- How do I respond when I feel under pressure or under attack?
- Do I want to stay in an argument and get it resolved, or do I want to flee and let everything blow over?

These questions are just the start of building your emotional intimacy. While it's easier to blame your spouse and say, "You are the reason I act like this," it is more helpful to realize the truth: that you each have your own patterns. Acknowledging your patterns first can become the catalyst for healing, connection, and the ability of your spouse to acknowledge their own patterns.

WHAT CAN I DO?

- Define what emotional intimacy means to you. One of the biggest challenges that individuals in a marriage face is that while you might be using the same words, you have different definitions. It might be a small difference but even the smallest differences in meaning can create disconnect.
- Find an emotion wheel and begin to identify what you are feeling in the moment. You can google "emotion wheel" or search on Amazon as there are many different ones. It's best to find one that is visually appealing to you. You may have to pull

out a dictionary or google a definition to make sure you know exactly what a word means. The bigger your emotional vocabulary is, the easier it will be to share with your spouse exactly what is going on with you.

- Identify how you would like your spouse to communicate with you. Would you like your spouse to ask if it's a good time to talk? Does it make it easier to understand what's going on if they give you all the background information or do you need them to get straight to the point? Does it matter to you if they interrupt to ask a question? Ask yourself, when do I feel the greatest willingness to engage in emotional intimacy?

WHAT CAN WE DO?

- Share the best ways to communicate and connect during the day. Is it easier to send text messages? Phone calls? FaceTime? Is it too busy in the morning or after work? What works for the two of you?
- Make it a priority to connect daily and weekly. Some suggestions: set a specific day/time on the calendar, sit together during your morning coffee, or at the table after dinner. Knowing that there's time to talk will bring security to the relationship. You won't be wondering when it *might happen,* you'll know when it is going to happen.

- Ask clarifying questions. Often when your spouse first starts to share something, especially if it's something that makes them sad or angry, there can be other emotions below the surface. Instead of responding to the first thing that they say, ask, can you give me more details on why you felt that way? You can always follow this up with "Tell me more about that." Or, "Why was that significant to you?" The more you know about what's going on with your spouse, the more you can connect with them to build your marriage.

TONY'S THOUGHTS

When Alisa would shut down, I felt frustrated, insignificant, and hurt. Here we were, in a moment of intense dialogue, only for me to then be shut out to figure out what was going on with her and how to fix the situation. It was irritating to deal with Alisa when she would get like this.

Nothing I did or said would break through the wall she had put up between us. I didn't understand why she wouldn't engage. My thoughts would run wild to the worst-case scenario of us getting divorced. Here was the love of my life, the woman I vowed to be married to until death do us part, and we couldn't even have a conversation anymore.

When she would shut down, it felt like she was saying my thoughts weren't important. It had to be her way or she would simply avoid the circumstances. It felt like manipulation or control.

What I had seen growing up was that if there was a

problem, it got dealt with. I grew up in a large Italian family where things got talked about. Based on the tone of voice, sometimes it was hard to tell if it was a discussion or a fight, and yet it never ended without some kind of resolution.

Being married to a woman who didn't deal with things in the same way was so difficult. What I didn't know was that she experienced something very different growing up. Shutting down was common in her household when an argument happened. These two differences determined how we would engage each other when we had our own misunderstandings.

Our argument dance continued for many years. The same outcome would happen time and time again. And then it hit us both. We were living our lives based on those we had seen while growing up. But this was *our* marriage, and we needed to strengthen our emotional intimacy.

This was the moment where each of us had to take responsibility for our own behaviors and actions toward one another. Believing that we could strengthen our emotional intimacy was the first step toward a healthy and thriving marriage.

It's been a journey to this place where our Emotional Intimacy Pillar is strong. You can do the same thing. The tools that we share have not only impacted our lives but thousands of other couples around the world. You can use them as well to strengthen your emotional intimacy.

With this awareness of emotional intimacy, let's talk about physical intimacy in the next chapter.

CHAPTER 6

PILLAR #2: PHYSICAL INTIMACY

Touch me when I ask. Touch me when I am afraid to ask. Also, touch me with your lips, your hands, your heart.

———

Anonymous

P hysical intimacy is another area that can trip couples up. Most people will use the phrase "physical intimacy" and "sexual intimacy" interchangeably, and yet these two intimacies are very different.

You can have physical intimacy without sexual intimacy, but it's virtually impossible to have sexual intimacy with your spouse without some aspect of physical intimacy.

Physical intimacy is the closeness and connection created through your loving touch. It could include holding hands, kisses, cuddles, back massages, foot rubs, or any other non-sexual touch that answers the question, "How do I like to be touched, and how does my spouse like to be touched?"

It's so fascinating to compare the early stages of our relationship to the early years of our marriage, especially after kids.

It took us a little over two weeks to go from meeting each other to our first kiss. The first summer that we were together we held hands, cuddled up together, and had our arms around one another whenever we were out. We were a couple who couldn't keep our hands off of one another.

Then came marriage and babies.

During the early years of marriage, our schedules had us on opposite shifts or working such long hours that we hardly had time together. Instead of cuddling up together on the couch, we'd sit on opposite sides of the couch so we could "veg out." Instead of giving a long hug or a deep kiss, we'd make do with a quick hug or a peck on the cheek. Our pillar of physical intimacy was in a slow decline.

That decline sped up with the birth of our children. Our

kids were born three years apart, and between being pregnant, breastfeeding, and having a toddler hanging all over me for the better part of six years, I felt completely touched out. In this season, Tony would randomly come to me and try to hug me or hold hands and I'd push him away, annoyed that one more person in the house wanted something from me. I struggled with wanting to give our kids hugs and kisses and being frustrated that Tony wanted the same from me. And at the time I didn't have the awareness of how to share this with Tony.

In the last chapter, I shared that the Emotional Intimacy Pillar is the workhorse of the 6 Pillars of Intimacy. Why is that? Because when you are dealing with any of the other five, like your Physical Intimacy Pillar, how you handle it often comes out in how you communicate. For example, when Tony would try to be physical with me in any way, I would often cry out: "Stop touching me! You don't know what it's like to have someone touching you all day long. I don't want you to touch me." On one particularly bad day, I just rolled my eyes and let out an enormous sigh. Definitely not a highlight of our marriage.

I did not know how much this pillar actually mattered.

What I didn't know was that for Tony, our physical intimacy conveys to him that he matters, that I see him and desire him, that he is important to me. When this pillar was cracked in our marriage, it was easy for him to think that the only thing that he was good for was being a provider and a dad. And while these things are important, it was more important to him that I see him as a man and as my husband first. Recognizing that his desire to be physically intimate didn't just go away because we had kids.

This was a *huge* struggle for us. When I would complain about feeling all "touched out," I felt like Tony was only trying to touch me because he wanted sex (which wasn't true). Neither of us knew how to verbalize that this pillar had cracks in it or how we wanted to be touched. We weren't talking about the problem or looking for a solution, we were only complaining about what was wrong.

He knew I was capable of physical connection, he saw it with the kids, he saw it when I easily hugged friends. These were very intentional actions. This meant that I had to bring that same level of intentionality to our marriage. I had to be intentional about touching him *and* be receptive to his touches. It's not a one-way street. I had to step into a place where we could talk about the touches that were meaningful to both of us. The more we were able to share, the more success we had.

I remember during the 60-Day Sex Challenge and even after that we had many conversations about the meaning of physical intimacy to Tony. Truthfully, this is still a conversation in our marriage today. For me, it's not an automatic response. I actually have to consciously think about touching him. Case in point, he loves to have my hand resting on his thigh when he's driving. When we sit in the car, this is what goes through my head:

1. Tony's driving.
2. He likes it when I reach out and rest my hand on his leg while he's driving.

3. Reach out and rest your hand on his leg.
4. Do it.

> Your body was designed to touch and be touched.

For me, it was taking the time to hear that this was so important to my husband and if it was important to him, I needed to find a way to make it work for both of us. Does he still find it weird that I have to think about it? Yes. But you know what, it's okay because when I do think about it, he gets what he wants: a wife who is able to be intimate in this way.

WHAT PHYSICAL INTIMACY CONVEYS

This pillar is important because of what physical touch can convey to another person. A loved one's touch, especially from your spouse, conveys security and belonging. It brings a sense of peace.

Your body was designed to touch and be touched. From the first moments a baby is born, parents and caregivers are encouraged to touch the baby to convey love and to nurture the baby. That doesn't end when we become adults. You were designed for physical intimacy with your spouse. Your bodies fit together. The motivation to be physically intimate comes from an innate desire to connect with your spouse.

Think back to when you were first getting to know each other. In most relationships, there was a special moment when you first held hands or kissed. There were hugs when greeting each other or when leaving. There was holding hands while walking through the park, or cuddling up on the couch.

Touch is often an integral part of the early phases of a relationship. It's often one of the first ways you express interest or desire. How did your bodies connect? What did it feel like to touch your love? How did their touch make you feel?

Over time, with kids, the stresses of life, different schedules, and more, your physical intimacy is often one of the first areas where couples experience disconnection. For example, perhaps you have noticed one or more of the following:

- Your kisses have gone from heart-racing make-out sessions to barely a peck on the cheek. 73 percent of self-reporting couples in the ONE Family said that their kisses are a quick peck![1]
- Where you once used to cuddle up on the couch to watch a movie, you now find yourselves on opposite ends with no touching at all.
- Instead of holding hands or wrapping your arms around one another, you walk side-by-side and don't touch at all.
- It feels weird to reach out and lay a hand or an arm on your spouse because of the tension between the two of you.

Without physical intimacy, your marriage can feel like a relationship between roommates. It's two people sharing the same house and the same responsibilities, and yet you have nothing that would differentiate yourselves as a married couple.

WHO, WHAT, WHEN, WHY, WHERE, AND HOW

WHO?

The two of you. You cannot have meaningful touch when you are by yourself. It's impossible to give yourself a hug or kiss yourself on the forehead. You aren't able to hold hands with yourself or give yourself a backrub. It takes two. When the two of you choose to engage in your Physical Intimacy Pillar, you are choosing to touch the person to whom you said, "I do." That's so important.

WHAT?

Some people like bear hugs and some people want their spouse to come up from behind and wrap them up in their arms. Others like back massages. Some like to have their feet rubbed and others like a good back rub. Holding hands makes some people feel connected, while others would rather have a kiss on their forehead. What touches matter most to you and your spouse?

Most folks don't realize that a person's preferred physical touch can change over time and in different seasons of marriage. What is significant to a new bride may not be the same for a mom of toddlers. What makes a husband feel connected when he's under stress may not be the same kinds of touches he desires most while on vacation. Learning what touches matter most to your spouse is a journey for the entirety of your marriage. Don't assume that what used to work still works. Have an ongoing conversation with your spouse about how you can create physical intimacy with them.

WHEN?

In every intimacy, timing is important. Physical intimacy is no different. When is it important for your spouse to feel physically connected to you? Is it that lingering hug or kiss before heading out to work? Does she like to cuddle before bed? Does he get a smile on his face when you hold hands while walking on the beach? Are there times when physical intimacy makes your spouse feel uncomfortable—perhaps in front of their parents or the kids? These are all questions to discuss with one another. Remember, the two of you are growing, changing people. When you like to be physical may ebb and flow over the course of your marriage. Nothing is set in stone.

> Loving touch reduces cortisol, the stress hormone, and increases oxytocin, the love hormone.

WHY?

One more reminder: your body and your spouse's body were both designed for touch. In a very real way, you never truly outgrow that need. It may look different over time, but it's still an important need. Physical intimacy does so much for your marriage. Loving touch reduces cortisol, the stress hormone, and increases oxytocin, the love hormone. Physical intimacy decreases stress levels.[2] Marriages in which physical intimacy is strong report increased satisfaction in both the marriage and in life.[3] Why? Because when you and your spouse are touching, there is a sense of belonging, of connection, of being each other's person. Touch becomes another way to communicate your love to your spouse. Think about it...in a world where most people are only comfortable with a handshake or a quick hug, physical touch between the two of you conveys a depth to the relationship that only the two of you have.

WHERE?

The "where" of physical intimacy can refer to two different things: where on your body do you like to be touched, and where, geographically, are you most comfortable engaging in physical intimacy?

Let's start with where on your body. Everyone is unique, which means there are unique, specific places on your body where touch brings heightened sensitivity and connection, and other places where, eh, not so much. The same is true of your spouse. Don't assume that just because you like to have a particular place on your body touched that your spouse does as well. Ask them, and honor what they say. I love having my head massaged—Tony, not so much. Tony loves it when I place my hand on his leg while he's driving. When I'm driving, his hand on my leg is not nearly as significant. Find out where your spouse likes to be touched—ask them directly. Don't guess.

As for locations, where you two can be physically intimate depends on the "what" and the "when." Some couples are comfortable being physically intimate no matter where they are, while others save it for their home. There is no right or wrong answer to where the two of you can be physically intimate with one another so long as you are safe and in a spot where it is legal to do so. What matters is that you discuss it and have a plan that works for your marriage.

HOW?

For some of you, it will be as simple as reaching out to touch your love. For others, it will begin with the conversation around touch. Based on what you have previously experienced in physical intimacy, there may be areas that need to be healed and worked through in order for this pillar to be strengthened in your marriage.

Everyone has a history when it comes to how you touch and how you have been touched. You are currently writing your present and your future. There's no need to complicate things. Start with where you are right now and take action.

A COMMON CHALLENGE:

"I'm not touchy feely."

Not everyone is. But let's not get so caught up in identity.

How do you want to show up in your marriage? For your spouse? Maybe you didn't grow up with parents who were physically affectionate, so you've never witnessed what that looked like, or maybe touch isn't as deep a need for you. You don't have to be "touchy feely" to have strong physical intimacy in your marriage. You don't need to be all over each other 24/7 for this pillar to be strong. The two of you can make this pillar strong by communicating and developing what works for you. Remember, there's no need to compare your marriage to others. Extraordinary couples figure out what works for them.

I work with many couples for whom this is a challenge. One story stands out:

This couple, married almost thirty years, came to coaching after an affair was discovered. They knew they didn't want to divorce but weren't sure if they could stay married. One of the biggest sticking points? For years, the wife had told her husband that she wasn't touchy feely. Touch didn't matter so much to her so she didn't consider it a necessity to give any form of physical intimacy to her husband. The problem was that he still wanted it and the absence of physical intimacy in the marriage had opened the door to another woman meeting that need.

In the process of rebuilding the marriage and restoring touch, the Physical Intimacy Pillar was one that we focused on. In coaching sessions, the wife finally understood what he had been asking for over all those years. It wasn't just the touch, it was her attention. He wanted to know that he was important to her. With this revelation she began the process of changing her mindset around touch. No longer was she focused on whether or not touch was important to her. For the sake of her marriage and the connection with her husband, she chose to engage in physical intimacy with her husband. Through her loving touch, he began to see just how much he meant to her. He saw the effort that she was making and it began the healing process. This couple has celebrated their 30th wedding anniversary, and today their marriage is fully restored. Their Physical Intimacy Pillar is one of their strongest because of what they learned about one another.

CRACKS IN YOUR PHYSICAL INTIMACY PILLAR

Physical intimacy can be an interesting pillar because you (or your spouse) can do just enough to make it *look* like you are okay here, but really the pillar has cracks. Ask yourself:

- What does it look like when the two of you kiss? Are there passionate kisses or do you typically just do a quick peck, if anything at all?
- Do you know how your spouse likes to be touched?
- Do you feel you have to beg your spouse to touch you?
- When you are sitting on the couch, are you sitting at opposite ends (or on two different couches) or are you right next to each other?
- Do you sleep in the same bed?
- Do you avoid touching your spouse?
- Does he/she avoid touching you?

As with any of the intimacies, you don't have to have all of these present in your marriage to have cracks in your pillar, and it's possible that the crack in your Physical Intimacy Pillar looks different from any of these listed. That doesn't mean you don't have to address it. Think about what could be possible for the two of you if you leveled up the physical intimacy in your marriage:

> **Physical intimacy doesn't have to be a casualty in a long marriage.**

- What if your kids were saying, "Get a room" because you couldn't keep your hands off each other?
- What if the passionate kisses you had in the beginning made a reappearance?
- What if you knew exactly how your spouse liked to be touched?
- What if your spouse knew how you like to be touched and acted on that information?
- What if you felt that sense of belonging or desire that can only be conveyed by the one you love?

Physical intimacy doesn't have to be a casualty in a long marriage. You don't have to expect it to fade away. It can be just as vital today as it was when you first met—if not, even better, because you have learned so much more about one another.

This testimony is from one of my clients who struggled with physical intimacy:

Over the years, I've struggled with having passionate kisses with my wife. We gave one another a peck here and there, yet a long kiss that we both indulged in hadn't been something we'd done in a very long time. I'm not even really sure when this changed. It just seemed like somewhere along the way with kids and work and being busy we stopped making time for this simple act of physical intimacy.

I decided to bring this up to my wife. We had a discussion around the roadblocks that have been stopping me from having long, passionate kisses with her. Alisa had shared the journey of the 60-Day of Sex Challenge, and we had talked about the book 7 Days of Sex Challenge in one of our sessions. I decided to modify the idea of the 7-Day Challenge for where we were and what I knew we needed to work on. I took a massive leap of faith and suggested we have a passionate kiss for seven days straight.

I'm pleased to say after a few days, I actually enjoyed kissing her. Thank you so much for giving us the tools we needed to make our physical intimacy pillar stronger. I'm looking forward to many more passionate and long kisses.

— T. P. (husband)

BABY STEPS

What does it look like to strengthen the physical intimacy in your marriage? Where can you start?

Start with yourself. Sometimes this pillar has a crack because you haven't taken the time to reflect on how your likes have changed over the course of your marriage.

Ask yourself:
- What touches do you like?
- What touches does he/she like?
- What can I do to touch my spouse in the way he/she likes?

Use these questions to get the conversation started. Building physical intimacy, like any of the intimacies, is a process. You aren't looking for the short-term answer, but rather the long-term solution that will work for the two of you.

WHAT CAN I DO?

- Answer the question when your spouse asks you how you like to be touched. It's okay to ask for some time to think about it, but don't just say, "I don't know." Your spouse can't do anything with that response. It leaves them feeling frustrated and helpless to meet your needs. Start with something, you can always revisit it.
- Be intentional about building physical intimacy with the touches that he/she likes. Create a list of the touches that he/she likes so that you aren't at a loss. Set an alarm on your phone reminding you to touch them.
- Say thank you when your spouse touches you in a way that you like. The simple act of expressing gratitude helps to create a positive cycle in your marriage (couldn't we all use more of that?). It enables your spouse to know that they have

touched you in a way that is meaningful. Everyone has a need to know that what they are doing is working. Let your spouse know.

WHAT CAN WE DO?

- Go on a touch scavenger hunt. Spend time touching one another's bodies with one purpose: to find out what feels good and what doesn't. This is an exercise that the two of you can come back to time and again. As bodies change, as kids grow, as you deal with medical conditions, etc., find out what works now. Don't make assumptions.
- Schedule time to hold each other. As I shared earlier in this chapter, touch reduces stress, lowers cortisol levels, and raises the levels of oxytocin. Given that most couples are go-go-go it's important to set aside time for this activity. You'd be amazed at how much can shift in as little as ten minutes.

TONY'S THOUGHTS

My beautiful wife, Alisa, has an incredible body, and I've always been attracted to her. From the first time I saw her to this day, I love holding her, holding hands with her, being close to her, and touching her. What didn't make sense to me was when she wasn't open to touch during different seasons in our marriage.

This began to reveal itself more once we had kids. It was then that I could see with my own eyes that touch could happen.

I would see her hugging and kissing the kids all day long, so why not me? What was it between us that created a crack in our physical intimacy?

Expectations. Yes, what we expected of each other when it came to our physical intimacy pushed us away from one another instead of drawing us closer.

I had my own expectations, and Alisa had hers. It wasn't that we didn't want to ever touch each other, it was that we didn't know what it looked like to be physically intimate with one another in ways that didn't lead to sex.

As we began to undertand that our physical intimacy could be solely for connection, without sex, this pillar began to strengthen. Alisa shared that my giving her a hug with no intention of having it going further was important to her.

On my side, I didn't need to hold hands or be touched 24/7, and yet if she would put her left hand on my right knee when we drove together it would mean everything to me.

Over the years, we've learned that going to bed naked at times enhances our physical intimacy even if we only touch for a little bit during the night. I'm grateful for the way we get to connect in our physical intimacy and yet continue to adjust during different seasons of our lives and marriage.

Now that you've had the chance to work on how the two of you connect emotionally and physically, let's talk about an area that most people never consider: financial intimacy.

CHAPTER 7

PILLAR #3: FINANCIAL INTIMACY

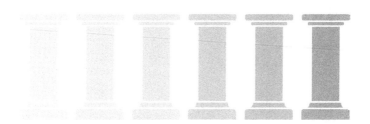

Money is an opportunity to reach unity in marriage. When couples work together they can do anything.

_____

Anonymous

I t's likely that some of you just laughed at reading the title of this chapter. Financial...intimacy? You might even ask yourself, "Is that even possible?"

Yes, it's possible. Not only that, it's actually *vital* for your marriage.

Financial intimacy is more than just, "We need to talk about the budget." It's about being close and connected in every financial aspect of your marriage. It's about having a plan for your day-to-day finances, but also your different accounts, insurances, plans for retirement, and the creation of an estate plan. Basically, if it has to do with money, it falls under the pillar of Financial Intimacy.

Sometimes for us, "money" and "marriage" have felt more like oil and water.

We've had a lot of challenges to our financial intimacy over the years. We started our marriage with over $50,000 in debt and dealt with collectors calling, consolidation, and finally working through Dave Ramsey's Financial Peace. You'd think it would have been smooth sailing after Financial Peace but...one Christmas, a year or two after we started ONE Extraordinary Marriage, I simply overspent. There were more than enough presents for everyone. I hadn't really paid attention to what was being purchased, and I truthfully ignored that gnawing feeling that I was spending too much.

I justified that the spending was to give the kids a great Christmas and to make sure that all our family had wonderful gifts. I didn't think about the long-term impact of my decisions. I was strictly living in the here-and-now with no regard for Tony.

Until we had to talk about our January budget.

At the beginning of every month, we sit down to discuss the bills that have to be paid. That January, I had to sit across the table from my husband and tell him that there was about $800 that wasn't available for the January budget, because I had spent it on Christmas presents.

I can still see the shocked look on his face and feel the lump in my stomach. Looking back, I can see the intersection of emotional and financial intimacy in that moment, but at the time I just felt nauseous.

At that moment, we had to get very real about our financial situation and we had to make some hard choices about spending, about our financial picture, and about the changes we were going to make.

We had to cut out all unnecessary spending. This meant eating out, Target runs, cable, Starbucks—anything that wasn't shelter, food, or utilities was gone. As a mom with two little kids, things got serious quickly! We had to make a lot of decisions on wants versus needs, and it turned out that a lot of what we were spending money on at the time was about wants. Our finances had to get back to being about needs.

It wasn't easy, but then issues about money often aren't easy for couples.

WHAT YOU BELIEVE ABOUT MONEY IMPACTS YOU AND YOUR MARRIAGE

Money is such an interesting topic because every single person has their own beliefs about money: what it is, how it works, and how you talk about it. These beliefs begin to be formed in childhood.

Right now, ask yourself what the money story was like in your family.

- Who handled the finances?
- Did you have more than enough? Just enough? Never enough?
- Did you see your parents save for what you needed, or did they just buy on impulse?
- Did you hear expressions like:
  - Money doesn't grow on trees.
  - We don't have money for that.
  - We can't afford that.
- Did your parents pay for everything, or did you have to work at an early age?
- Did you witness financial stress coming from a job loss, the death of a loved one, bankruptcy, repossession, or foreclosure?

You might think these questions aren't that big of a deal, but the truth is, they are impacting the two of you right now. If his dad always handled the money and never consulted his mom, you might have the answer as to why your husband never asks for your financial input and handles everything himself. If her mom didn't trust her dad to take care of the family finances, it could be the reason why she always seems to be questioning your choices. If he grew up with "never enough" it may explain why he doesn't want to spend money on anything for the two of you. If she never heard the word "no" when it came to the things that she wanted growing up, it could be why the two of you battle over every purchase. More times than not, I've seen that couples struggling with financial intimacy are dealing with beliefs that have been around for a long time in both of their lives.

It's rare for both spouses to come to the marriage without some sort of money "baggage" from past experiences and money behaviors that may not work together. How you come into your marriage will most definitely affect your marriage once the two of you bring your money together. Financial intimacy isn't automatic for everyone. A lifetime of behaviors can have you not sure how to address this particular pillar.

For me, I had a lot of financial insecurity based on life circumstances. When I was a senior in high school, my parents went through bankruptcy and ultimately lost our home right before I left for college. I remember having the church deliver a turkey dinner for Thanksgiving but being too embarrassed to even answer the door. Because of these experiences, I've always wanted us to have money in the bank, *and* I've wanted to make sure that our kids have never had the same experience. These mindsets impacted how Tony and I connected on our financial intimacy. It wasn't until I understood how to be vulnerable in this area, that we could truly be intimate and share.

WHO, WHAT, WHEN, WHY, WHERE, AND HOW

WHO?

The two of you. It doesn't matter if you have joint accounts or separate accounts. It doesn't matter if one of you is a stay-at-home parent and one is in the workplace, or if you're both working. Financial intimacy in marriage isn't just one person's responsibility. Both of you have a role in knowing about the finances in your marriage.

My urging on this comes from personal experience. Early in our marriage I worked for a bank and started to see this pattern. Older bank customers would come in with tears in their eyes. When asked what was wrong, they would explain that their spouse had died and they had no clue about the money, insurance, or any of their accounts. They were literally blind to their financial picture at a time when they were most vulnerable. Please get involved in the financial aspect of your marriage. You cannot afford not to.

> **Both of you have a role in knowing about the finances in your marriage.**

The two of you may find that in different seasons, one spouse or the other takes the lead in specific areas. You might find that one of you prefers to pay the monthly bills or has greater skill in that area. Whereas the other might choose to handle insurance, investments, and retirement. One of you might take the lead on getting the taxes done, while the other is all about saving for the next trip, big purchase, or college account. It's okay to have the roles change over the course of the marriage; remember the two of you are in this together.

WHAT?

A lot of people think that financial intimacy is simply working on the budget (or cash flow plan if you don't like the word budget). And while that's one aspect of your financial intimacy, it's not everything. Pause for a second and think about all the areas impacted by your finances:

- Insurance
- Retirement
- College funds
- Mortgage
- Investments
- Vacations
- And more

Financial intimacy is everything from knowing your passwords and who your financial advisors/representatives are to planning your monthly cash flow, discussing retirement, and putting together your estate plan. It's not just talking about the bills that come in; it's developing a shared language in your marriage around finances. It's choosing to be knowledgeable in this area of your relationship.

WHEN?

Financial intimacy, just like all the intimacies, is strongest when there is regular conversation around this area. Some aspects you will discuss daily or weekly, some monthly or quarterly and some annually. The two of you ought to discuss the budget, at minimum, on a monthly basis. You should have conversations about purchases—weekly, if needed—in order to make sure the two of you are on the same page and staying within what you can afford. When it comes time to renew your insurance plan, review your coverages together; typically, this is an annual review. Revisit your estate plan every five years or when you've experienced a major life transition like buying a home (or selling one), having kids, becoming empty nesters or retirement. Financial intimacy isn't one of those things that you set up and forget about for the rest of your life. Just like the two of you are growing and changing, so does your financial life.

WHY?

Most individuals come into marriage with a specific mindset around money, and often with a bit of financial baggage. Building a strong pillar of financial intimacy requires you to unpack your financial mindset and baggage. Until you get to the root of why you think and act how you do regarding money, you'll find the same cycles and conflicts repeating themselves, often creating frustration in your marriage. True financial intimacy allows the two of you to work together, with understanding and grace, to achieve your financial goals as a team.

The two of you chose to build a life together. Embracing financial intimacy is one aspect of that life. It's not something that can be effectively relegated to the side.

WHERE?

For some of you, you'll sit at the table or at the computer discussing the monthly cash flow plan (or "budget," if you prefer). For others, this will mean using the same app so the two of you can be on the same page in real time. It's likely that there will be an annual conversation with your insurance agent and/or financial advisor to make sure everything is on track.

If you have found that there are some locations, maybe the dining room table or in the kitchen, where the financial conversations seem to be in a broken cycle, it's okay to change where you discuss your financial intimacy. There is no rule that says it has to be done in the same place it's always been done.

> **Finances will always be a part of your marriage, so expect that there will be many conversations, not just one.**

HOW?

Start small. Don't try to tackle every aspect of your financial intimacy in one conversation. Finances will always be a part of your marriage, so expect that there will be many conversations, not just one. Learn about your spouse's financial upbringing. Ask questions to understand what the roles looked like in their family and what they expect in your marriage. Share responsibilities. Even if one person is primarily responsible for financial decisions, you should both know where to access the information. When there is financial intimacy, there is a tremendous amount of security in the relationship.

Here's the story of a couple that I've had the privilege to coach. As newlyweds, they had both come into the marriage with their own money and chose to keep everything separate. They pooled a certain amount of money each month for the household needs but everything else was separate. They figured it was easiest this way. That was until the unknown spending habits started to impact the two of them. Debt was being racked up; creditors were calling. They didn't know what the other was doing until the damage was done. There had been no financial intimacy and this almost destroyed their young marriage.

As part of the work that we did together, they decided to open a joint checking account and to put all their money *in one account*. This was uncomfortable for both of them. It was a new level of vulnerability and awareness in their marriage. It made them responsible to one another. It forced conversations around purchases and created a transparency they hadn't had before. As they chose to work together, they found it became easier the more that they engaged with one another.

A COMMON CHALLENGE:

"I'm not comfortable with money or talking about money."

Join the club. Money is one of those topics that is not often discussed "around the kids," so it's likely you didn't get a chance to witness your parents working through financial challenges or developing financial intimacy. Every family handles money differently and passes along different messages about money and financial resources to their children. You may also find that if one of you doesn't have a paycheck it can be hard to talk about your finances. I hear from a lot of coaching clients, "I can't say anything about how we spend money; I'm not the one who makes it."

It's important to identify what makes you uncomfortable:

> The only way to get comfortable with the uncomfortable is to practice.

- I've never talked about money.
- I don't have a head for numbers.
- I'm not good at sticking to a budget.
- I don't know how much we spend.
- I've never had to manage my finances.
- Or maybe something else.

Share what actually makes you uncomfortable with your spouse so that the two of you can address this as a team. The only way to get comfortable with the uncomfortable is to practice. Make a commitment to strengthen this muscle. Develop a plan that includes a time and a place to discuss your financial intimacy; remember to start small.

CRACKS IN YOUR FINANCIAL INTIMACY PILLAR

Money baggage and behaviors like these can cause your Financial Intimacy Pillar to crack:

- Credit card secrets or hiding purchases, such as playing the credit card shuffle or leaving purchases in the car so you can bring them in over time (one in three couples who fight about money have hidden a purchase).[1]

- Overspending. For some, this will be hundreds of dollars—for others, thousands or tens of thousands.
- Not having a discussion around the budget, financial needs, or concerns. Forty-three percent of couples struggle to stick to a budget that is kept by both spouses.[1]
- Carrying debt on credit cards, student loans, or business loans. According to a study by Ramsey Financial Solutions, 86 percent of marriages less than five years old started with debt. In forty-eight percent of those marriages, the debt is more than $50,000. Money is the number one cause of fights.[1]
- Only one of you has access or knows the passwords to all of your accounts. This is a lack of financial intimacy, and it shows a lack of transparency and accessibility in the marriage.
- There isn't a plan for big purchases, college, or retirement.
- Avoiding estate planning because it's uncomfortable or you don't want to think about it. Estimates are that only 32 percent of Americans have a will, which means that 68 percent of people will allow the courts to decide what happens to their assets upon death.[2]

But what could the two of you accomplish, if:

- Each month, you prepared a budget/cash flow plan and lived within it?
- You had a plan to get out of debt?

- You invested together for short-term and long-term goals?
- You both knew where all the accounts and passwords were located?
- You conducted monthly or quarterly and annual reviews of your financial wellbeing?
- You created an estate plan, so that you both knew how you were going to handle things in the event of illness or death?

Strengthening your financial intimacy is so important because:

- 94 percent of those who defined their marriage as "great" discuss their money.[1]
- 54 percent who say they have a "great" marriage are almost twice as likely to talk about money daily or weekly.[1]

Move yourself into a place where you are creating a great marriage by developing intimacy in this area.

This testimony is from a client who struggled with financial intimacy in his marriage:

Over the years, our financial intimacy has ebbed and flowed. Sometimes we were doing amazing, and other times we had to press in to pay off debt, save, and prepare for our future. My wife and I have been married for over thirty years, and I've always been the one to handle our finances, investments, insurance, you name it.

Recently, I completed something I'd been intending to do for some time: I wrote a letter to my wife, detailing our finances and investments in the case of my death.

We're not getting any younger and we've seen many of our friends begin to die. I've read about this kind of letter and heard it recommended, but I just never chose to do it until today. It's weird to put something together that you know will only be used after you're gone, but I'm so glad that I did it. She's more confident now about her situation, should something happen to me. That's a big win for our financial intimacy. She's got a peace of mind that even in death, I'm taking care of her. Neither one of us really wants to think about our death but more importantly, I didn't want to think about her struggling to find all of this as she was grieving. I realized I did this for both of us.

— T. S. (husband)

BABY STEPS

A strong Financial Intimacy Pillar starts with looking at your finances and your relationship to money. Ask yourself:

- How comfortable am I with discussing money?
- What are my mindsets around money?
- What is one thing we could do to strengthen this pillar?

Make the time to self reflect, then share with your spouse.

WHAT CAN I DO?

- Be transparent in your purchases. It's time to stop leaving things in the trunk or rounding down on

how much you spent so that it sounds better.
- Participate in financial conversations with your spouse. Being a participant means that you share your thoughts. You acknowledge what you are feeling and you work with your spouse to find unity.

WHAT CAN WE DO?

- Honor agreed-upon spending limits. If the two of you have established that any purchase over a certain dollar amount gets an okay from your spouse, follow through. For example, Tony and I have a standing agreement that outside of groceries, if we are looking at a purchase that's over $200, we will check in with one another. This has been a flexible number in our marriage as our finances have changed. But the commitment to honor this number keeps us from having budgetary surprises.
- Review credit reports annually. Doing an annual review of your credit reports allows the two of you to make sure that everything is accurate and that nothing has been placed on your reports in error. Strong credit is important for a lot of different activities like buying a car or buying/ refinancing a home. The two of you don't want any surprises.
- Make an appointment to get your estate plan, including a will, in place. I know that no one

likes to talk about death or dying, but knowing that you have these documents prepared brings such a measure of peace. I actually looked at Tony after we signed our documents and said, "It's okay if you die now." Why? I felt secure in knowing our finances were being taken care of and that I understood his wishes.

TONY'S THOUGHTS

Reflecting on the story that Alisa shared at the beginning of the chapter, we jokingly refer to that Christmas as "The Christmas She Overspent." I still remember sitting at the table as she started to tell me about the money we didn't have and all I could think was, "This can't be happening. I've been working to make ends meet so we could have some semblance of a Christmas and Alisa goes and spends money we don't have on Christmas presents. Are you kidding me?"

I couldn't believe it. At the time I was the sole provider as we had decided that she would stay home with the kids. Each month we would sit down and look over our cash flow plan (our budget). I trusted her to stay within the plan that we had for each other. I trusted her to tell me what was going on with our finances, and if she was going to make any adjustments.

What she had done felt like such a betrayal of everything that we had been doing to strengthen our financial intimacy. There was a rather large crack in our Financial Intimacy Pillar.

At this point, I immediately began to think about and share all the things we were going to have to cut out of the cash flow plan in order to make it so that we could pay all our bills. Being in this spot scared me like I've never been before. There were times when I was paralyzed by what could happen, and yet in this moment I went into overdrive "fix it" mode.

Instead of just talking once a month about what we were spending or what was coming up, I made sure that we were checking in weekly and sometimes even daily. This wasn't about control, it was about us coming together as a team to strengthen our financial intimacy.

The Great Recession had to be one of the most stressful times that we faced in our finances. It was through this refining time that we had to be vigilant about our cash flow plan that has allowed us to prosper in ways that we would have never believed before.

As you learn to build your financial intimacy, you will develop the skills needed to address another intimacy: spiritual intimacy.

CHAPTER 8

PILLAR #4: SPIRITUAL INTIMACY

Our faith becomes stronger as we express it.

Billy Graham

Although we often explore our own spiritual needs, we rarely stop to think about those same needs as it applies to being a couple. When times get tough, your faith and your marriage will be the foundation that you need to get through it all.

You may have heard sermon messages about couples praying together or sharing their faith. However, you may have wondered what that looked like or how you can step into creating this intimacy in your marriage.

Spiritual intimacy encompasses all your religious beliefs and observed religious practices. This can be as simple as praying together, going to church together, or discussing spiritual issues as a couple. In some ways, this pillar can be more intimate than sex!

We both grew up Catholic and, for different reasons, stopped attending church or practicing faith in our teenage years. We got married by a Methodist minister at a winery. It was definitely not the Catholic wedding that either of our families had hoped for. The only reason we chose that minister was because the winery recommended him as an officiant who was familiar with the venue.

In the early years of our marriage, we didn't really discuss faith, religion, or spirituality. It was a non-factor in our marriage until Tony hiked the Pacific Crest Trail from Mexico to Canada in 2000.

While Tony was hiking, I had an encounter that can only be described as miraculous. Around midnight one night, I heard banging on my front door and male voices swearing. Instead of calling 911, I ran to the front door and looked out the peephole. As I stood at the door I could see three drunk men trying to get in the door. I knew that they had the wrong apartment but they were too drunk to notice. I was so scared that something would happen to me if they managed to break down the door. As I stood staring through the peephole and praying they wouldn't make it in, I heard a voice behind me saying, "This isn't your apartment." The men looked up, realized their mistake, and left, laughing. The only thing keeping them out of the apartment was the chain at the top of the door. To this day, I am convinced that the voice that we all heard was an angel, as there was definitely no one else in our apartment.

At almost the same time, Tony was having his own spiritual experience on the trail. As we shared these encounters via our infrequent phone calls it was clear that something was changing in our marriage. There was a shift happening in how the two of us were connecting. It was a new level.

Upon Tony's return home, we began attending church together. Something we had *never* done in all our years of marriage. We found ourselves praying for one another and reading the Bible. We began looking for devotionals to do together and had worship music playing in our home and car. This was just the beginning of developing our spiritual intimacy.

Spiritual intimacy is an area of life that most consider very individual. However, in a marriage, if you are dealing with something, your spouse is too. That is true even in this area of spiritual intimacy.

Being able to talk about your faith in God, share your

faith struggles, or simply just worship together can be ways for couples to find connection, feel supported, and feel in alignment with one another.

I said earlier in this chapter that sometimes spiritual intimacy can actually feel more vulnerable and intimate than sexual intimacy. Let's expand on that a bit more.

SPIRITUAL INTIMACY CAN BE MORE INTIMATE THAN SEX

When you hear your spouse praying or worshipping, you are able to see them in a different light. It's more than just checking a box to go to Sunday service or sending up a "Dear God, thank you for this food." When you choose to become spiritually intimate through prayer, discussing their burdens, what they are struggling with, and what they are asking God for—you are getting a literal window into their soul. Most people never share their prayers with another person.

Think about how you pray and what you pray for. Sometimes you pray out of joy and sometimes out of grief. There are situations in which your heart is breaking and you are praying for relief. At other times, you are praying for comfort and peace. In certain circumstances you are praying earnestly for breakthrough or provision. And chances are good you've prayed a prayer or two out of gratitude.

These are different areas of your life that matter to you and yet—does your spouse know how much they matter to you? What are you willing to say when it's just you? How do you cry out to God? Many people will use that time to release some of the strongest emotions like: anger, frustration, sadness, or grief. But what happens when you open the door to sharing this with your spouse and building your spiritual intimacy?

When you stand together in prayer you are activating your faith and coming in agreement with one another. As Matthew 18:19 says, "...truly I tell you that if two of you on earth agree about anything they ask for, it will be done for them by my Father in heaven." Your spoken prayers have the power to shift what's happening in you, your spouse, and your marriage. Praying aloud and together is powerful. It's a way of connecting your hearts and recentering your marriage. This shared experience enables you to support each other as you collectively believe and release those things not in your control.

Prayer alone is powerful. Praying together magnifies the stabilizing, powerful feelings because you are doing it as a unified team. In Ecclesiastes 4:12, we are reminded that, "Though one may be overpowered, two can defend themselves. A cord of three strands is not quickly broken." Choosing to be spiritually intimate with your spouse, is building a supernatural strength against all the attacks on your marriage.

WHO, WHAT, WHEN, WHY, WHERE, AND HOW

WHO?

No surprise here. It's you and your spouse. Together. The two of you are on this journey together. Regardless of what you have learned about spirituality in the past, spiritual intimacy within a marriage takes two people to be real and vulnerable with one another. It's important to know what's going on spiritually with yourself and with your spouse.

WHAT?

The activities that the two of you engage in will be unique to your marriage. Such activities may include:

- Attending church service together (in person or online).
- Worshipping together. This can be during a service or even just through having worship music playing in your home.
- Praying with one another and for one another, because you've had conversations and know what is going on in your spouse's life. Sometimes you may find that your spouse needs you to pray for them because they cannot do it themselves.
- Attending a small group/connect group/home group. It's one thing to have friends; it's another thing to "do life" with people, to share your vulnerabilities, and to allow them to pray for you and see the real you.
- Tithing to your church.
- Something else altogether. You won't know the "what" until the two of you have a conversation about this.

WHEN?

Maybe it's a weekend service or a midweek service. For some, it will be a devotional every morning. For others, it will be praying before the two of you go to bed every night. The two of you will determine the "when," as a team, by finding a rhythm that works for your marriage.

WHY?

Research has shown that in couples who have been married for more than two decades, one of the most important qualities they found was "faith in God and spiritual commitment."[1] A relationship with God provides couples with a shared sense of values, ideology, and purpose.

> A relationship with God provides couples with a shared sense of values, ideology, and purpose.

More than the shared values and purpose, being spiritually intimate is a choice to share your soul with another person. It's sharing the most intimate wishes, desires, and struggles. It's trusting your spouse with your heart and your faith.

WHERE?

It could be your church, your car, or your home. You might feel closest to God walking on the beach, hiking in the mountains or sitting by the lake. The two of you can worship and pray together in a lot of different settings. Where do you feel closest to God? Where do the two of you feel safest in sharing your spiritual intimacy? This doesn't have to look the same for you as it does for other people. Your spiritual intimacy is not necessarily confined to a particular space.

HOW?

The "how" starts with understanding how *you* practice your spirituality. What is it you do regularly? Do you pray? Is attending services important to you? Do you like to have worship music playing at home or in the car? Where can you invite your spouse to join you?

You can begin by sharing where you are in your faith journey. What were the messages you received growing up about faith, and about sharing your faith with others? Developing this intimacy may require you to first understand your own relationship to your faith.

A COMMON CHALLENGE:

"We struggle to pray together."

I hear ya! This has been a challenge for Tony and me as well. From our earliest years in church, it seemed like every pastor was talking about getting up before the crack of dawn to pray with their spouse for an hour. Truthfully, this was probably just my perception of what they were saying, but ultimately it seemed unattainable and we felt like failures. Tony and I would try and get up early and pray only to decide that sleep was a better option. Then we tried doing it at night and that was also met with the same sleep challenge.

Like any area of your marriage, it's important for the two of you to find a rhythm that works for you because for some couples first thing in the morning or at the very end of the day works for them.

When the two of you say that you want to pray together, what does this mean? Does it mean that you want to pray together every day or once a week? Does it mean that you are using a devotional or that you are reading the Bible together or you are sitting on your bed praying together?

There is no wrong way for a couple to pray together. What matters is that the two of you are choosing to share with your spouse what is going on inside you spiritually, you are choosing vulnerability. Don't worry about what other people are doing, start with where the two of you are right now and build on that.

CRACKS IN YOUR SPIRITUAL INTIMACY PILLAR

Spiritual intimacy is a pillar that can often feel shaky, or like it has cracks in it. This is often because of one's upbringing, or the church telling you that your relationship with God is yours and no one else's. But, as in Mark 10:8, "For this reason a man will leave his father and his mother, and be united to his wife, and they will become one flesh."

Becoming one isn't just about the areas of your marriage that are easy or "normal" to share. It's about sharing all of yourselves, including your spiritual intimacy.

This pillar can have cracks in it when you have:

- Difficulty praying together because it feels awkward or vulnerable, or maybe because you've never prayed out loud with another person before.
- Concerns over sharing faith practices.
- Made the choice not to go to services together because one of you doesn't feel comfortable in the church or isn't interested in attending church.
- Discomfort in bringing up faith or spiritual matters to your spouse.
- Factors in play like inconsistency, comfort levels, expectations, and feeling vulnerable.

Below is a testimony from one of my clients who struggled with spiritual intimacy:

Faith has been a source of tension from time to time in our marriage. Over the years, I've struggled with not being spiritually intimate with my husband. I've wanted us to do more things spiritually, together but that's not comfortable for him. He was raised with the belief that your relationship with God is private—not something to be shared or discussed.

Since finding The 6 Pillars of Intimacy *and* ONE Extraordinary Marriage Show, *my faith has deepened in ways I never would have expected. I remember listening early on about how you came up with the name "ONE." Listening to you talk about Scripture made me read the Song of Solomon, and I was hooked!* (I shared the story behind the name ONE in A Quick Note at the beginning of the book.)

Even if my husband doesn't connect in the same way, my relationship with God has strengthened our marriage in significant ways. I've made praying for my husband a regular part of my day. I regularly ask him how I can be praying for him. While he may not choose for us to pray together, this regular conversation is opening the door to us being able to connect spiritually.

— M. H. (wife)

BABY STEPS

Deepening your spiritual intimacy doesn't "just happen." Like every intimacy, it starts with asking a few questions:

- When I think of spiritual intimacy, what comes to mind?
- How comfortable am I with discussing faith, religion, or spirituality with my spouse?
- What is one way we can be spiritually intimate with one another?

WHAT CAN I DO?

- Pray for your spouse. Praying for your spouse requires you to know what is going on with them. The only way to know what's going on is to ask questions and listen. It's building emotional intimacy and spiritual intimacy at the same time.
- Encourage your spouse on their spiritual journey. The two of you may not be at the same

place at the same time. How can you encourage your spouse with where they are now?

WHAT CAN WE DO?

- Attend services together. Any time that you are able to share an experience with your spouse, you are building intimacy. Choose to go to your services together. Be mindful of your attitude about going and how that is being conveyed to your spouse.
- Pray *with* your spouse. Praying, out loud, with another person, is a very intimate exercise. Hearing their vulnerabilities and concerns, what they are praying for and what they are declaring provide insight into situations in their life and how they are processing them.

> Any time that you are able to share an experience with your spouse, you are building intimacy.

- Study the Bible or a devotional together. When the two of you choose to read the same material and then discuss it, you are afforded an opportunity to learn how your spouse thinks and what affects them.

TONY'S THOUGHTS

Faith was a non-entity when we first met and into the early years of our marriage. We were living our life how we wanted without any focus on our spiritual intimacy. There were times when it would get brought up—usually at Christmas and Easter when my mom and aunt would ask us to attend church services with them.

Other than those two occasions each year, the thought of attending church or having a relationship with our Heavenly Father was relatively nonexistent, except when Alisa's parents would come to visit. My father-in-law, no matter where he was, would find the closest Catholic church so he could attend Mass.

Between our third and fourth year of marriage, I stepped onto the Pacific Crest Trail to thru-hike (an end-to-end backpacking trip on a long-distance trail) from Mexico to Canada. Before I left, my amazing mother-in-law sent me the Footprints poem.

One night a man had a dream. He dreamed he was walking along the beach with the LORD.

Across the sky flashed scenes from his life. For each scene he noticed two sets of footprints in the sand: one belonging to him, and the other to the LORD.

When the last scene of his life flashed before him, he looked back at the footprints in the sand.

He noticed that many times along the path of his life there was only one set of footprints.

He also noticed that it happened at the very lowest and saddest times in his life.

This really bothered him and he questioned the LORD about it:

"LORD, you said that once I decided to follow you, you'd walk with me all the way. But I have noticed that during the most troublesome times in my life, there is only one set of footprints. I don't understand why when I needed you most you would leave me."

The LORD replied:

"My son, my precious child, I love you and I would never leave you. During your times of trial and suffering, when you see only one set of footprints, it was then that I carried you."

From the start of my hike on the Pacific Crest Trail, this poem became my bedtime ritual. As I'd lay out my sleeping bag to settle in for the night and write in my journal, I'd pick up the bookmark and read it to myself.

What began to strike me was that there were many times throughout my day when I felt alone. The Pacific Crest Trail runs 2,658 miles, and I was hiking on average twenty miles a day. There is a lot of time to think as I covered the many different landscapes the west has to offer.

Five hundred miles into my hike, I met another thru-hiker, nicknamed Arkansas Dave. Yes, he was from Arkansas. We ended up hiking almost two thousand miles together and had a lot of time to contemplate life. One evening while we were camping on the flanks of Mt. Jefferson in Oregon, our conversation turned to the Bible.

As we talked about faith and a relationship with Jesus he tossed me a Bible and said, "Read John."

This was a turning point in my spiritual journey.

As Alisa shared she was having her own spiritual journey, which opened up the door for us to have our first true conversations about faith. Did everything change overnight? No. It's been a twenty-plus-year journey of learning to be spiritually intimate with one another. Like all the intimacies, we've had to be intentional and take action to strengthen this pillar through all seasons of our marriage.

As you grow in your spiritual intimacy, you'll find that there are new or unique ways for the two of you to spend time together. Couples need to spend time together in order to stay in love and grow their marriage as we will discuss in the next chapter on recreational intimacy.

CHAPTER 9

PILLAR #5: RECREATIONAL INTIMACY

Planning is bringing the future into the present so that you can do something about it now.

———

Alan Lakein

We can see a few of you scratching your head right now. The last two chapters dealt with financial intimacy and spiritual intimacy, which were likely two concepts that—while they might not have made total sense before reading the chapters—you were probably familiar with.

But recreational intimacy? What the heck is this?

We're glad you asked. Recreational intimacy is all about what you do together at home, on dates, or just for fun. It's the plans the two of you make to spend time together, doing things you enjoy, having fun.

Spending time together and having fun isn't just reserved for when you were dating, or as newlyweds. It's possible to not only spend time together after you've been married a while, but to really enjoy it.

How many of you have had this happen in your marriage? It's date night. The two of you are sitting in the driveway. If you have little kids who need a sitter, the sitter is already on the clock, charging you for her time.

You're about to pull out of the driveway when one looks to the other and says, "Where do you want to go?"

"I don't know," the other replies. "Where do you want to go?"

"It doesn't really matter to me, I'm fine with whatever you want."

"Awesome, let's go get pizza."

"Ugh...I don't really want pizza."

"I thought you said you didn't care what we did."

"I don't care what we do, but I don't want pizza."

"That doesn't make any sense."

Both of you roll your eyes, let out a gigantic sigh, and wonder why you even thought that going on a date was a good idea.

Or maybe you didn't even get that far. Maybe you thought about going on a date, but realized all you would have done was head to the same restaurant where you always go, order the same food you always get (why mess with a good thing?), and have the same conversations that you always have. It's about as appealing as going to wait at the DMV.

But what if spending time together could be something that you enjoy? What if you could break out of the routines and have fun? Please tell me you still want to have fun!

FUN DOESN'T STOP AFTER THE "I DO"

Fun is not something that needs to stop after the wedding, or after kids, or when you've landed that dream job. Just because you are a married adult doesn't mean that you aren't allowed to have fun. Married couples can laugh together. They can do things that bring them joy. Nowhere is it written that married couples have to be dull and boring and do the same things all the time.

Having fun is actually one of the healthiest things that you can do for yourself and for your marriage. When you engage in fun activities you decrease your levels of cortisol, the stress hormone and increase your serotonin levels which can help your mood and your sleep.[1] Having fun encourages creativity and productivity, both of which can be incredibly beneficial in a marriage.[2]

Think about your fondest childhood memories, then stop and allow yourself to find ways in your marriage to make that level of fun happen, adult style. We all need to laugh more, and we all need to do things that bring us joy. If you're not having fun, then it's time to step back, regroup, and find what's making you enjoy life less than you should be. Go for a skinny dip, watch cartoons, drink coffee together, and play hide and seek with one another. Invite fun into your marriage and watch what happens to your connection.

> Dates with your children are not dates; those are called family outings. Please don't confuse the two.

WHO, WHAT, WHEN, WHY, WHERE, AND HOW

WHO?

You and your spouse. You need to spend time, *quality* time, with your spouse. We've said it before, and we'll say it again: the two of you are growing, changing people. Spending time with your spouse one-on-one allows you to learn who they are now and what matters to them. Time spent with other people *and* your spouse is not necessarily recreational intimacy if you are more focused on all the other people who are around you. Dates with your children are not dates; those are called family outings. Please don't confuse the two.

WHAT?

Recreational intimacy covers everything from dates to shared activities. Some couples will garden together, some will go ice fishing, others will take dance lessons, and others will cook gourmet meals together. What you choose to do will be as unique as the two of you. Building strength in the Recreational Intimacy Pillar means you won't always do the same thing every single time. Rather, the two of you will develop the ability to not only try new things, but also to ask *and answer* the question, "What would you like to do?" and then go do it. This also means that sometimes you may not be super excited about what your spouse is suggesting...my advice: Unless it's something illegal or just an absolute **NO** for you, try it. You might just find something that you like.

Here's the story of one of my coaching clients:

This couple had married later in life and were quite set in their ways. They liked what they liked and weren't necessarily open to trying new things. During their courtship season, they had generally kept to "safe" experiences—things that they knew the other liked to do. They each had very separate interests and were content to give each other space to do those things.

After the wedding they found that those separate interests, and more importantly the time spent doing them was causing tension in the marriage. They found themselves having arguments that sounded like this:

"You're spending too much time watching the Nascar races. It seems like it's every weekend."

"I don't know why this is such a big deal; you're always wanting to go to the shooting range."

"You said that you didn't care about me doing that. Why is this coming up now?"

"It just seems like you'd rather be there than with me!"

"I'd rather be with you, but you're not interested in this. You never want to go with me."

"I only said one time that I didn't want to go and you've never asked me again."

It turns out that those interests would actually make for some incredible experiences for this couple. She invited him to go to a Nascar race, and he offered to take her to the shooting range. He now follows a different driver, and it turns out that she's pretty good with a gun. Those different experiences actually became a catalyst for new memories and strengthening their marriage.

WHEN?

As often as you can. For so many couples, recreational intimacy becomes the glue that holds them together (remember: it's time together, new experiences, and memory building). It's the quick coffee dates. It's finding a new restaurant. It's taking a walk around the lake. It's dating with intention, long after you've said "I do." Get your time together on the calendar so that you aren't leaving it to chance or hoping you'll find the time. Prioritize time spent together so you get refreshed and recharged...together.

Keep in mind that this intimacy may look different in different seasons of marriage. What the two of you can do as a couple without kids looks very different from what you can do as a couple with toddlers or even as empty-nesters. How you can spend time together during busy work seasons differs from when you are on vacation. It is important to recognize the season that you are in and to adjust your expectations accordingly. This doesn't mean that you put recreational intimacy "on hold;" it just means that you have to work with the season you are in to keep this pillar strong.

WHY?

It's not only fashionable to say "go on dates," it's statistically beneficial for the two of you. Researchers have found that married couples who go on frequent dates and take part in activities together have a lower divorce rate, and feel better about the quality of their marriage.[3] Couples who spend time together weekly are 3.5 times more likely to report being happy in their relationship.[4] Couples who date regularly, even just once a month, can lower their chances of divorce by 14 percent.[5]

Over time, you both can get caught up in the "busyness" of life. The conversations about going on a date or doing a fun activity together dwindle, and you miss out on time for the two of you to connect.

It's easy to think, "We'll be able to spend time together later, when we're not so busy, after the kids grow up, when work lets up." But it's the time that you invest now in one another that actually matters to the health of your marriage. You cannot keep waiting for that magic, perfect moment to spend time together. An extraordinary marriage is built upon investing lots of little pockets of time focused on one another, really seeing and getting to know the other person.

The two of you need to keep having fun beyond the dating season. Life can get serious quickly after the wedding. You find yourselves with bills to pay, kids to raise, and a host of other obligations. When you make recreational intimacy a focus, you are showing to your spouse that time *with them* is important to you.

WHERE?

Anywhere the two of you can spend time together and give one another your attention. It doesn't matter what you are doing as long as you are doing something together, fully engaged with one another. Some suggestions:

- Take a helicopter or hot-air-balloon ride
- Play a game at your kitchen table
- Go axe throwing
- Go apple or berry picking
- Make a romantic dinner together
- Attend a comedy show
- Show off your karaoke skills
- Go stargazing in your backyard
- Sit at the beach, by the lake, or in the park

When the two of you are focused on one another, anywhere can be a place to deepen your recreational intimacy.

HOW?

Start with getting time with your spouse on the calendar. Yes, schedule time with your love. Don't let other things come in the way of the two of you spending time together. I often tell coaching clients that you should treat that time with your spouse like a doctor's appointment. You know how hard it is to get on a doctor's calendar, and you know that if you have to reschedule it could take months to find another appointment. Time with your spouse should be that important. Get it scheduled. It's okay to schedule the time. You know that all of the important things in your life get on your calendar. If you claim that your marriage is important, don't neglect to put this on the calendar.

Have conversations about what you like to do and what you would like to try. Just because one of you used to like to do something doesn't mean that you still like doing it. Remember, when you try something new, you create new memories. It breaks the two of you out of your routines and creates higher levels of engagement in the marriage.

One way to do this: Each of you grab a sheet of paper and write the numbers 1–5 on the paper. Pick a theme for your time together; for example, you might write down date nights at home, ideas for a lazy Saturday or date night ideas under $20. Each of you, independently, write down ideas that *you* would get excited about. When done, the two of you swap lists. You now have a list of winning ideas that your spouse would get excited about. Go make it happen!

A COMMON CHALLENGE:

"I'm always the one to plan the dates. It makes me not want to do it."

This is a common complaint in recreational intimacy, and it's one that can easily be shifted. Think back to when you were dating. There's a high likelihood that you both planned activities, many of which were new to you or your spouse. It's time for both of you to embrace that sense of adventure again.

If you are the spouse who always plans the dates, ask your spouse why they never plan a date. There can be many reasons for this, and we have solutions for some of the top reasons here:

1. "You never like the dates that I plan." If your spouse has repeatedly tried to plan dates and you never like what he/she does, it's time to pull out that list of winning ideas you just put together. When it's your turn to plan a date, pick something from your spouse's list, put your own spin on it, and make the decision that you are going to make the best of this new adventure.

2. "We never have time for dates." Put yourselves on the calendar first. You are the two most important people in your marriage. Don't have so many other activities or people on your calendar that you don't have time for one another. Start with the two of you, and then allow other things onto your calendar.

3. "I don't know the contact info for the sitter, or how to set up a sitter." For those of you who have kids,

this can be a common issue. Have a conversation about how this is going to get handled. We have a teenage daughter, so we understand how weird it would be if an adult man started texting her, even if it was to set up a babysitting job. The two of you need to address your workaround. Does the wife confirm the date with the sitter, and then he plans the rest? Do the two of you have a regular date on the calendar so you always know you have a sitter, and then you take turns planning the date? Or is there another solution for the babysitter question?

As with any aspect of intimacy, recreational intimacy is not just one person's responsibility. There are two of you in the marriage, and it takes two to spend time with one another.

CRACKS IN YOUR RECREATIONAL INTIMACY PILLAR

> Don't let your past patterns dictate the present.

Spending time together and having fun can take a backseat to the things that you "have to" do. It's easy to feel like everyone and everything else is so important, but sometimes you have to say no to other people or obligations, so you can say yes to one another. If you never put one another first, you will end up with cracks in your recreational intimacy.

You know you have cracks in your Recreational Intimacy Pillar when:

- You can't remember the last time you went on a date.
- You use the common excuses like "We're too busy," or "We have kids."
- A fun activity together is rare or nonexistent. It's all about getting stuff done, not so much about keeping the spark alive in the marriage.
- The dates you do go on always look the same (same place, same meal, same conversations).
- One of you always seems to end up planning the time together, or else it doesn't happen.

Don't let your past patterns dictate the present. You can address these cracks to make change.

Here's what one couple had to say about what happened once they strengthened their Recreational Intimacy Pillar:

We had the chance to go skiing/snowboarding this weekend—just the two of us. My husband has been trying to get me out there for at least two years, if not more. I struggle when we are out there because my husband is so much better at it than I am. I usually feel like I am holding him back and keeping him from having fun. Even though I had said yes, I was trying to think of ways not to go up until the last minute.

I'm so glad that I went! All the work that we have been doing on the 6 Pillars of Intimacy, and especially our recreational intimacy, is paying off. Throughout the day, I would fall and my husband would be there helping me up.

We had a fun time doing something that he loves to do!

It's so hard for me to get out of my head and out of my comfort zone, but seeing the effects it has on my husband is amazing. I can tell by his actions that he definitely appreciates it. He is much more affectionate, happy, and helpful. But you know what? It wasn't just about him. I realized that there are things that I say no to that I might actually enjoy. I think I say no because it's easier, because it means that I don't have to try new things or get out of my comfort zone. This was such an eye-opening experience for both of us. I understand that if we are always doing the same thing that it's boring, and I don't want a boring marriage! I am so glad I got on the slopes with him. Our relationship feels brand new and refreshed!

— T. S. (wife)

YOUR SPOUSE IS ALWAYS CHANGING AND GROWING

Your spouse is always changing and growing. The person he/she was when the two of you got married may not be the same person now. The same goes for what he/she likes to do or wants to explore. You, too, are not the same person you were when you got married. Your likes have changed, just like your spouse's have. What you want to do or explore could be different. You cannot expect this area of your marriage to stay the same, or for you or your spouse to always like the same things.

BABY STEPS

Recreational intimacy requires you reflect on:
- What activities interest you in this season of life?
- What activities would you like to do together?
- How does it make you feel when you spend time together doing fun activities?

WHAT CAN I DO?

- Protect date time with your spouse. Everyone wants to feel important, especially the person that you are married to. Protecting this time means not cancelling if your friends want to go out or you just "don't feel like it." It means being intentional with your time so that you can be there and be present with your love.
- Choose to try things your spouse likes. You are married to someone who is different from you. This means they like different things and have different interests. Spending time with your spouse doing things that they like to do demonstrates your interest in who they are. You just might find something new that you enjoy.

> When the two of you are spending time together, be fully present.

- Put your phone down when spending time together. Your spouse wants your attention, your presence. When the two of you are spending time together, be fully present.

WHAT CAN WE DO?

- Be intentional about getting away; spending time outside of your home, just the two of you, is a major reset for your marriage. It's easy to get distracted with chores or the kids or even just other things to do when you are at home. When you become intentional about your Recreational Intimacy, it gives the two of you time to simply focus on each other and your marriage.

- Get creative in your time together. Who says that dates have to always be in the evening? Who says that time together should be dinner and a movie? It's your marriage, get creative in what you are going to do and when you are going to do it. You make the rules!

TONY'S THOUGHTS

From going on dates to fun activities we've done together, our Recreational Intimacy Pillar has been one that we've had to strengthen again and again. In the early years of marriage, we'd go to our local pizza shop every Friday night to decompress after a long week.

This turned into our hiking season where every weekend we'd find a new place to go adventure together. We'd go to our local sporting goods place on a Friday night to pick up last minute items for a day hike or weekend backpacking trip.

As we began to have kids, this pillar took a hit and cracks were revealed that we needed to address. During this season of life, instead of heading out for a date night, we'd get the kids to bed and then have quiet, candlelight dinners on our living room floor. Those were some fun times.

Kayaking, beach walks, day trips, drives up the coast, playing board or card games and other activities have been part of what we've done to strengthen our recreational intimacy. Each has brought us closer together to work together and to enjoy each other's company.

Busyness is a real enemy of marriage. You can be so busy spending your time doing other things and being with other people (kids, friends, co-workers) that there's no time for your spouse. If there's no time to be with them, it's very hard to stay in love with them. After a while you don't know who they are or what they like.

Time together is the antidote for that.

New experiences are the other ingredient in recreational intimacy. Routines are great in a lot of areas of your life. A morning routine helps you get to work on time without having to put too much mental energy into it. Your bedtime routine allows you to go on autopilot as your day winds down. Your marriage benefits when you are mentally involved and not on autopilot, new experiences encourage both of those. This doesn't mean that you have to do something new every time the two of you are spending time together, just think variety.

Recreational intimacy allows the two of you to work on many other intimacies while spending time together and having fun. As you invest in this time together, it's natural to see your sexual intimacy grow as well; let's talk about that next.

CHAPTER 10

PILLAR #6: SEXUAL INTIMACY

The more connections you and your lover make, not just between your bodies, but between your minds, your hearts and your souls, the more you will strengthen the fabric of your relationship and the more real moments you will experience together.

Barbara De Angelis

This is likely the pillar that you thought would start the 6 Pillars of Intimacy. As we shared with you in the early chapters, intimacy is often thought of as synonymous with the word "sex," but as you've seen over the last five chapters, there is so much more to intimacy than just sex.

There's no two ways about it: sex is important to your marriage.

However, that doesn't mean that we can or will ignore the importance of the Sexual Intimacy Pillar in your marriage. We start with the other five because when those are strong, this pillar has the potential to become exceptional.

Sexual intimacy encompasses everything about your sexual connection with your spouse. This can be, but is not limited to: romance, initiation, foreplay, and sexual intercourse itself. There's no two ways about it: sex is important to your marriage.

But sexual intimacy goes way beyond, "Hey, want to have sex?"

That line was spoken many times in our marriage, which lead to rejection, pity sex, and lackluster sexual encounters with one another. Sexual intimacy was a struggle in our marriage for almost a decade. Beyond having children, there were a couple other key factors that wreaked havoc on how the two of us connected in this pillar.

For me, all eleven years of Catholic education definitely impacted the early years of our marriage. As a girl, it seemed like the church, school, and even well-meaning adults had taught that sex was something dirty, that shouldn't be enjoyed, and that it was only about making babies. After getting married, I didn't know how to reconcile those thoughts with Tony's desire to have sex because we were married. I wrestled with guilt about having sex before marriage. If sex was dirty then why were there times that I enjoyed it? So much confusion and no answers. It wasn't long after we got married that we went from having frequent sex at all times of the day and night, trying new positions, and feeling comfortable talking about sex to having sex only at night, in the dark, rather infrequently, and in the missionary position—every time.

We argued about everything having to do with sex, including:

- Frequency
- Variety
- Initiation
- Foreplay
- Using toys
- Differences in desire

We didn't know how to express ourselves sexually, or how to talk about sex in a healthy way. We didn't know what it looked like for a couple to have a healthy sex life.

For most, this isn't something that your parents discussed with you as a teenager or young adult. One day you find yourself married, with the expectation that the sex is going to be wonderful after you say "I do." But what happens when it isn't?

Tony came into our marriage with an addiction to

pornography that had begun when he was twelve years old. This changed his perceptions of and expectations for sex and what it should be. I knew about the pornography when we got married, but I had no idea how much it would impact the two of us. Because of the pornography, I often felt in the early years of our marriage like Tony only needed a warm body to have sex, that it wouldn't have mattered who was there. This led to a lack of confidence on my part and a lack of interest in sex. Sex became a tug-of-war in our marriage.

The more he wanted it, the more I dug my heels in and pushed back, choosing not to have sex with him. Over the years, I came up with every excuse in the book not to have sex, I became the Queen of Rejection. I would say things like:

- I'm too tired.
- I have a headache.
- I have cramps.
- I don't feel like it.
- I have to fold laundry/wash dishes/clean up.
- I don't want the kids to hear us.
- One of the kids needs me.

Eventually, I would just get tired of him asking and say, "Fine, let's have sex." But I wasn't engaged. I wasn't mentally there. I was just waiting for him to get done so I could be done. There was no romance in our marriage. There was no initiating on my part. If we were going to have sex, Tony was going to have to make the moves. There was little to no foreplay, which often meant that sex was uncomfortable for both of us. Sex, which is supposed to be this beautiful experience in marriage, was simply another task on the to-do list.

We didn't understand that sexual intimacy strengthens your emotional connection and heightens your trust in each other. The benefits of having sex regularly go beyond the emotional connection; regular sex has been linked to living longer, better heart health, lower stress levels and higher self-esteem.[1] We wanted all of that, we just didn't know how to get it.

THE BEST SEX ED

Developing sexual intimacy starts with understanding your body and your spouse's body. Most of us had a health class that touched on the male and female reproductive systems. It was great anatomical knowledge—at one point, I could probably label all the body parts but I couldn't have told you how they work. I knew from sex ed what an erection was and how a baby was made, but the practical application was a bit different.

Being sexually intimate with another person isn't just inserting his penis into her vagina. It's learning how your bodies really work, how arousal impacts his body and her body. It's understanding the different touches that create a response. It's understanding natural lubrication and menstrual cycles. It's learning how to engage one another mentally and physically in order to create a sexual response.[2,3]

Psalm 139:14 says "... I am fearfully and wonderfully made..." Your body is amazing and so is your spouse's body. Marriage is a life-long course in sex ed because your body and your responses will change over the years. What works when you are in your 20s might not work in your 50s. Her body after kids will respond differently than it did before kids. Illness and medication will impact arousal and responses. Learning what works is a lifetime adventure for the two of you, and it's not just about what's happening sexually.

Strengthening your sexual intimacy also means educating yourself on what's happening with your spouse emotionally. What happens in your head can have just as much of an impact on your sexual intimacy as what happens below the belt. Worry, anxiety, fear, resentment—these can all impact the depth of your sexual intimacy. When you become aware that these are a factor in your sexual intimacy, it's key to get help to work through them. You want to keep learning and growing together.

> Learning what works is a lifetime adventure for the two of you, and it's not just about what's happening sexually.

WHO, WHAT, WHEN, WHY, WHERE, AND HOW

WHO?

No surprise here, it's the two of you. And *only* the two of you. Sexual acts done by yourself, or with someone who is not your spouse, do not build the sexual intimacy in your marriage. It's the two of you engaging in behavior that, within the marriage covenant, is only meant for the two of you.

To be blunt, open marriages, swinging, affairs, etc., any way in which another person could be invited into your marriage *does not* build sexual intimacy. As a coach, I have seen too many situations in which it was believed that the introduction of another person into the marriage would be beneficial only to have it create jealousy, insecurity, and low self-esteem. The risks far exceed any idealized reward.

WHAT?

Any sexual act that deepens your connection with your spouse. This isn't just sexual intercourse. Sexual intimacy includes intercourse along with romance, how you initiate, and even foreplay. It's not just the act itself, it's the interaction the two of you have before, during, and after.

Quick note on how we define the difference between initiating sex and foreplay. Initiating sex is everything that you do that is an overture to the two of you being sexually intimate. It might be sending a sexy text early in the morning hinting at what's to come or leaving a special piece of lingerie on the bed. It's all of the actions before the two of you get to the point of being together for sexual intimacy. Foreplay is all of the actions between the two of you prior to sexual intercourse. This can include making out, massages, rubbing one another, and oral sex. There can be times when initiating sex is foreplay, but not always.

We have said, from the beginning of ONE Extraordinary Marriage, that you only go as far as you and your spouse are comfortable. If one of you suggests something that the other is not comfortable with, that's a no-go. Do not force your spouse to have sex with you or engage in acts that make them feel less than or uncomfortable.

It's important for me to address pornography and erotica in this section. Pornography and erotica change your perception of what is expected or accepted in the bedroom. Together they create a false narrative around sexual behaviors and can have one spouse feeling insecure or inadequate.[4] I have coached too many couples whose marriage has been devastated by either one of these to not address it here.

WHEN?

Whenever you want! There is no rule that says sexual intimacy can only happen at night or at the end of the day. There are twenty-four hours in every day, so you have lots of time to be sexually intimate. Morning sex is amazing, because you aren't overwhelmed or exhausted by all the tasks of the day. Daytime sex means that you can enjoy one another fully awake, and still go to bed on time. You can flirt with one another throughout the day in anticipation of connecting later on. Try different times of day to see how it affects your sexual intimacy.

Since we're talking about the "when," we should note that it's also important to make sexual intimacy a priority on your calendar. Yes, we are talking about scheduling that time with your spouse. This doesn't mean that you have to have "Friday at 9:07 p.m." set aside on the calendar, but rather that you have marked days or weeks when you take turns initiating and making your sexual intimacy a priority. We've shared this concept of scheduling sex for the last eleven years, and it has changed marriages around the world. When sex is on the calendar, there is no more guessing if, *or when,* it's going to happen. You need to be as intentional about this intimacy as you are about any of them.

WHY?

Sexual intimacy has the ability to connect the two of you—mind, body, and soul. It's more than just a physical release; it's an opportunity for the two of you to experience one another in a way that is completely vulnerable and completely open.

WHERE?

> Sexual intimacy has the ability to connect the two of you—mind, body, and soul.

Your bed is the obvious answer, but that's not the only place that the two of you can be sexually intimate. Your home has multiple rooms. You can use any of them for sexual intimacy. Think shower, laundry or even the kitchen.

You're not limited to your house, either. Couples have had sex in their cars (yes, married couples do this) as well as in the outdoors. Here are a few locations that have been shared with us over the years:

- On a trampoline
- Down a dark road
- In the ocean
- In the cornfields
- On the top of a fire truck

Just remember to obey all local laws regarding sex outside of your home.

HOW?

Well, this is where emotional intimacy joins with sexual intimacy. A lot of couples will default to the missionary position because they don't ever really talk about their sexual intimacy. They don't know what they would like to try regarding lubes, toys, or positions. As the two of you are building your 6 Pillars of Intimacy and, specifically, your sexual intimacy, you will develop the ability to talk about what you like or would like to try. The two of you will understand how you both initiate so signals aren't missed. You'll create a marriage in which sex is something you both look forward to, because you know each of your needs will be met. Sex won't be one-sided, because it will become a pillar of intimacy that the two of you have intentionally built.

A COMMON CHALLENGE:

"I don't want to schedule sex. I want it to be spontaneous."

This is probably the number one statement we hear when it comes to being intentional about sexual intimacy. People worry that if they talk about it, get intentional, and even schedule sex that it will become mechanical or robotic, lacking all creativity. The funny thing is that when we ask people how often they are having spontaneous sex, most people don't have an answer—because they aren't.

We get it. We know you enjoy variety and creativity, and that's actually the beauty of being intentional about your sexual intimacy. As you have more conversations with your spouse and learn what works for them, for you, and what the two of you would like to explore together, you'll find more fulfillment in this intimacy.

When you know that sex is on the calendar, it builds anticipation. It allows the two of you to brainstorm creative ideas because you know it's coming. Don't let your preconceived notions about scheduling sexual intimacy keep you from experiencing what's possible when the two of you are on the same page.

> What's going on in one's sex life can indicate other challenges a marriage is facing.

Scheduling sex is good for both the high-desire and the low-desire spouse. Differences in desire often exist in a marriage, and it's not always the man who has the higher desire. Knowing that sexual intimacy is scheduled eases the concern of the high-desire spouse from wondering when it will happen. For the low-desire spouse, knowing that sex is scheduled allows them time to mentally prepare for that time together. Scheduling sex sets the expectations for both spouses.

CRACKS IN YOUR SEXUAL INTIMACY PILLAR

This pillar is often used as a barometer for the health of the relationship. What's going on in one's sex life can indicate other challenges a marriage is facing. When you feel disconnected in your sexual intimacy, you definitely want to address those cracks.

These cracks can include:

- You can't remember the last time you had sex (or enjoyed it). A sexless marriage is defined as one in which there are fewer than ten encounters in a year.[5]
- Sex feels like something on the "To Do" list, because there are so many other things that the two of you are responsible for, and there are only so many hours in the day. It feels more like checking a box than any type of meaningful encounter.
- Sexual rejection happens often in your marriage. This isn't the occasional no, it's the repeated rejection of advances by one spouse.
- You struggle to bring up your needs or desires because you don't know how your spouse is going to respond, and you worry about judgment.
- It's become a routine, doing the same position at the same time of day. For a lot of couples, this means that while they are physically present, mentally, they are not.

Here's a testimonial from a coaching client who struggled with this pillar:

When I married my wife I had been struggling with porn for many years. On top of that, we both felt guilty for having sex outside of marriage. Our premarital course didn't really talk about sexual intimacy, and within one to two years of our marriage I came to the conclusion that our sex life was just going to stay broken because of past choices. I no longer would bring up my desires as my wife would become annoyed and disgusted with the requests.

Over the years, I broke trust with her many times by turning to porn to take care of my needs. Last year, after I confessed about the porn again, she told me that she needed time to evaluate our marriage and her desire to stay in. It was then that I knew I had to take action.

I began working on myself, connecting with her emotionally and spiritually. As she began to see the changes take place—and holding, she slowly opened herself up to me, and our sexual intimacy began to change.

Last night, my wife rolled over in bed, woke me up, and initiated spontaneously, out of the blue at 10:30 at night! This has never happened before in twelve years of marriage. What's even more incredible is that this is in the midst of a family member living with us. This morning when I asked my wife what flipped a switch for her last night, she responded "it's even more important now that we be intentional in our marriage." Couldn't agree more!

After ten years of a subpar, survival-mode, roommate-syndrome marriage, I cannot be more in love with my wife.

— M.M. (husband)

BABY STEPS

Developing healthy sexual intimacy begins with simple conversations between the two of you. Start with answering questions like:

- What would a healthy sex life look like for the two of you?
- Does your spouse know what you like or would like to try?
- What are the desires that you have never expressed with one another?

From here you can begin the journey of learning who the two of you are and how you can strengthen your sexual intimacy.

WHAT CAN I DO?

- Romance your spouse. Everyone likes to feel special and desired. What this means for you and your spouse is likely different. Some people like flowers or a love note. Others want a massage or a phone call. It's important to know what makes your spouse feel desired as desire plays a key role in your sexual intimacy.

- Find out what color your spouse likes to see you wearing. It might seem that talking about favorite colors is a bit childish, but hold on. Men and women are visual creatures. Color impacts our mood, our feelings and even our confidence. When you know what color your spouse likes to see you wearing, you can pick out the lingerie or underwear especially for them. Knowing that you are wearing their favorite color, in anticipation of something happening, will create arousal in you, and once they find out, arousal in them.

- Vocalize during sex. Voicing your pleasure during sex is a way of communicating to your spouse your pleasure. In many instances you both may have your eyes shut, vocalizations become another way to share what you are feeling.

WHAT CAN WE DO?

- Try lubricant. Lubrication is a gift to both of you. No one likes to go down a dry water slide. The same is true in your marriage, that much friction is not your friend. Wives, there may be times during your cycle when you need the extra moisture. This can also happen as a result of medications or menopause. If the two of you are trying to have a quickie, your body may not have time to naturally lubricate. Don't have uncomfortable sex. Use lube.

- Make your bedroom a no-rejection zone. This doesn't mean you always have to say yes if your spouse wants to have sex. It means the two of you build your emotional intimacy to the point that you know what is going on in your spouse's life, and you have a schedule for your sexual intimacy, so you don't have to say no.

- Make sex a priority in your marriage. Sex is good for you. It's important to the bond the two of you have. Move from making it the last thing on the to-do list to an important priority. Schedule it. Talk about it. Be present during it. All of these will contribute to feelings of deeper sexual intimacy.

TONY'S THOUGHTS

As I look back over our marriage, I believe that both Alisa and I fell into a place where we lacked sexual confidence. Sexual confidence was a challenge for us because we were just "supposed to figure it out" from the time we got married.

Well, we didn't.

The truth is, no one really talked to us about what it would look like to truly be sexually intimate. This led to cracks in our Sexual Intimacy Pillar that lasted for many years. Rejection, apathy, lack of desire, and disconnect on both of our parts kept us at an arm's length away.

Since that time, I have learned that sexual confidence is a feeling of self-assurance arising from one's appreciation of one's own abilities. Developing confidence takes time and practice, it's not something that just "happens." You have to work at it.

Over the years, as we became intentional in our sexual intimacy, our confidence helped us strengthen this pillar. We had to step into places that we hadn't in the past. We had to engage one another in those areas where we had emotionally hurt one another.

Even today, I've come to understand that my confidence in the bedroom is also dependent on how I open up and continue to be vulnerable to Alisa. Because the dynamic between the two of us is a living, breathing connection that is constantly growing, we can learn how to support each other to strengthen our sexual intimacy.

Staying vigilant when it comes to each of the 6 Pillars of Intimacy can help you both explore and support each other through these seasons where confidence is tough.

You may find that things that worked in the past don't work now. That's when it's important to communicate and support each other. Understanding where you struggle with confidence allows you to create a plan both individually and as a couple.

Knowledge is power, and learning what areas need to be strengthened equips the two of you to get on the same team to build your sexual confidence. Now that we have talked about the 6 Pillars of Intimacy, let's talk about how they work together in the next chapter.

CHAPTER 11

EVERY PILLAR MATTERS

Watch your thoughts, they become words. Watch your words, they become actions. Make sure to watch your actions because they become habits. Watch your habits, they become character. Watch your character, it becomes your destiny.

———————

Anonymous

We know that a lot of you are thinking, "Okay, if we can just fix whichever one of the 6 Pillars of Intimacy that has the most cracks, we'll be just fine."

Yes and no.

Remember how we described the pillars in Chapter 4? Pillars provide strength, add beauty, and carry weight.

Working on one pillar is a great place to start, but you cannot support the structure that is your marriage with only one or two strong pillars. You need them all to have an extraordinary marriage. Think about what would happen to the roof of a building if its pillars were missing or had deep cracks. The roof would collapse, and people would get hurt.

The same is true if you ignore the fact that every one of the six pillars matters. Every marriage will go through seasons: the newlywed phase, kids (if you have them), aging, illness, grief, loss. In some seasons you may find that certain pillars are weaker than in other seasons.

For example:

- When our son Andrew died in 2004, our emotional intimacy tanked. I couldn't talk without crying. I couldn't wrap my head around what happened. I felt depressed and withdrawn. We were truly co-existing with little else. There was no physical intimacy or sexual intimacy as well. The one pillar that kept us going in that season—spiritual intimacy. I remember us praying for our son to live. I remember making it to church even when I didn't know if I'd be able to sit through an entire service. It took working through the grief to rebuild the emotional, physical, and sexual intimacy pillars.

- In 2012, we lost our home as a result of the Great Recession. The stress on our financial intimacy impacted our sexual intimacy. Even though we were scheduling sex, it was harder to connect and be fully present. It wasn't until we addressed the financial insecurity that we were able to reconnect sexually.

- During the years that our kids were in elementary and junior high school so much of our time revolved around their activities and their needs. If we weren't careful, this "busyness" would take a toll on our emotional and recreational intimacy. We had to fight against the "busyness" trap and put our marriage on the calendar first.

- In 2017, we were dealing with Tony's dad's declining health. We were having many conversations and staying emotionally connected. During that time, Tony shared that he needed more sexual intimacy as a way to stay connected and just be fully in the moment. It wasn't what I would have thought, but I understood that he needed that pillar to be stronger for a season.

When you develop skills in one intimacy, you can apply them to every other intimacy.

Every pillar matters.

All 6 Pillars of Intimacy are the secret to an extraordinary marriage—and here's where it gets exciting! When you develop skills in one intimacy, you can apply them to the other intimacies.

I had a couple in coaching years ago who were incredibly strong in their financial intimacy. The two of them could talk about budgets and retirement plans and life insurance with ease. There was total agreement when it came to being financially responsible and planning for the future.

But their sexual intimacy? *Crickets!*

Nothing.

Nada.

No conversations.

No connection.

Zip.

Zilch.

In a coaching session, they went into detail about some of their financial conversations. These conversations were uncomfortable, and both said it was hard, but in these tough conversations, they had learned to listen to one another, share their feelings, compromise, and create a game plan for their finances. They recognized they had survived the tough conversations and even learned how to work together.

It was an "Aha" moment. If they could do it with their finances, why couldn't they do it with their sexual intimacy? Why couldn't they create a regular time and place to discuss it? Or try different strategies like scheduling sex, taking turns initiating, and even having sex during the day to see what would work for them? Why couldn't they come up with a game plan, just like they had with their finances?

Nothing shifted until the moment they realized their skills in another intimacy could transfer to their sexual intimacy. They knew they had a "game plan" for their finances—who would handle what, how often they would check in with each other and what their commitments were to one another. Couldn't those same skills transfer to their sexual intimacy? Yes, with some subtle adjustments. With their sexual intimacy, they made a plan to take turns initiating sex, they both learned how to romance one another, and they scheduled time to not only have sex but to talk about what was working for them. They were empowered to make this pillar strong, and it changed dramatically for the two of them. No longer were they fighting over their sexual intimacy, together they were making it extraordinary!

You have skills. As you have read about the 6 Pillars of Intimacy, there have likely been one or two, or maybe more, where you have thought, "This is the one we are better at." It doesn't have to be perfect, or even super strong. All you need to do is think, "This is where we can start from."

THINK ABOUT THIS

Scenario #1:

A couple that has strong recreational intimacy has cultivated variety in the things that they do together. They have discovered how to handle the unexpected on adventures. They have developed the ability to navigate changes to itineraries. They are comfortable in new situations. If this can be done in their recreational intimacy, what would it look like for their financial intimacy, or sexual intimacy?

For their financial intimacy, they might look at new apps to track their spending or create a separate savings account for their dream vacations. They would have a willingness to discuss their comfort level with financial risk or uncertainty. When an unexpected bill comes in they work together to find a solution.

When it comes to sexual intimacy, they could try new positions or even new toys with the understanding that nothing they explore has to be a "forever" part of their sexual intimacy. When a position doesn't quite work the way they expect it to, they have the ability to communicate what's happening in such a way that their spouse understands that it's not about them but about the position.

Scenario #2:

A couple that is strong in their spiritual intimacy has learned to be real and vulnerable. They have developed the ability to express themselves in front of each other and communicate what is happening to them spiritually. If they can do this with their spiritual intimacy, how can they bring these same skills into their emotional intimacy or physical intimacy?

To build emotional intimacy, they can be intentional about making time to talk about their feelings or concerns.

They can carry the safety they have when praying together into the "hard conversations." When you know that you can trust your spouse with your prayers, you can also trust them with your feelings.

With their physical intimacy, they can choose to be vulnerable about the touches that are significant to them and the ones that aren't. A couple can develop the skills to talk about how their bodies are changing and what they need physically in a particular season.

Scenario #3:

A couple that is strong in their sexual intimacy has learned to create a safe space for themselves and their spouse. They have developed the ability to communicate their needs and desires in an area that is considered extremely sensitive. They embrace variety and creativity. If they can do this with their sexual intimacy, how could they bring these same skills to their spiritual intimacy or recreational intimacy?

> You and your spouse both have strengths.

In the same way that they are able to be vulnerable about their needs or desires sexually, they can share in regard to their spiritual needs. What are the deepest desires of their hearts? What have they not been able to share with anyone else?

When it comes to their recreational intimacy, they have the skills to share what excites them or concerns them about trying something new. They are able to get creative and break out of the routines for dates or activities. Their time together is not routine or boring.

A WORD ABOUT YOUR STRENGTHS...

You and your spouse both have strengths. You may wish that your spouse was strong in the same way you are, but chances are high that your strengths are different and that is a good thing. Don't minimize your spouse's strengths. What they bring to the marriage is important. Don't judge their strengths either. A strength is not good or bad. If it's not the same as yours, that simply means that it's different. Instead of judging how good or bad their strength is, judge how effectively the two of you are using your combined strengths to create an extraordinary marriage.

CHAPTER 12

THE FORK IN THE ROAD

Instead of being a product of my circumstances, I am a product of my decisions.

——————

Stephen Covey

This is the last chapter. You're at the end of the book. You're standing at the fork in the road. Which way will you go?

OPTION ONE: "THIS WAS A NICE BOOK."

Some of you will simply finish this book, think it was nice, put it on the bookshelf, and keep doing what you've been doing. We're glad that you read the book, but you know what? Things won't change if all you do is read this book. You'll continue to do what you've done, and the distance between the two of you will continue to grow.

Some of you will keep wishing for an answer, or you'll read more books and listen to more podcasts, hoping and wishing that someone will give you the magic wand or the fairy dust to make your marriage extraordinary. You'll keep dreaming of what your marriage could be, but you won't do anything to make that dream a reality.

OPTION TWO: "IT'S TIME TO TAKE ACTION!"

What if this is the breakthrough that will shift your marriage? What if this is what's been missing in your marriage? What if you could take this framework, take this knowledge, and create an extraordinary marriage?

It can be all these things. But it's up to you.

Knowledge without action is merely information. In our hyper-information world, you can Google the term "change my marriage" and get around 2,520,000,000 results. That's a lot. But you already knew that there was a lot of information available.

The secret to creating an extraordinary marriage is not solely information: it is deciding to take action, instead of waiting and hoping for something else to do it for you. It's taking the knowledge that you have gained and putting it into action, embracing the mindset that you can create change. It's understanding that you are an active participant in your marriage. You aren't just sitting by waiting for something to change; you are taking action to create change.

What does this look like?

- Start by identifying the pillar with the greatest strength in your marriage. Don't guess! Take *The 6 Pillars of Intimacy Quiz* (oneextraordinarymarriage.com/quiz) and acknowledge what is strong right now.
  - We ask you to identify what's strong because where you currently have strengths, you have skills. You figured out how to work together in that way. Knowing that you have been able to figure out one area allows you to apply that knowledge to the other intimacies.
- Identify the pillar that can have the greatest transformation. Again, use the results from your 6 Pillars of Intimacy Quiz. The pillar that has the lowest score has the greatest opportunity for breakthrough. Remember, you have shown strength in at least one of your intimacies. It's time to take those skills and apply them to this intimacy.
- Focus first on "What Can I Do?" Every change

in marriage starts with each spouse taking responsibility for their actions. Don't wait for your spouse to take action. Get in the game. Take action.

- Then take action on "What Can We Do?" You both have strengths you bring to the marriage. Your marriage needs all of those strengths. When you work together, you can create something greater than you could ever imagine. Focusing on the strengths shifts how you see your spouse and your marriage.

Side note on the quiz: any quiz is simply a snapshot in time. You base your feelings about your marriage on how you feel about yourself, your spouse, and your marriage dynamic when you take the quiz. It's not an identity. It simply provides understanding.

Be intentional to fight back from roommate syndrome. Take action to change the direction of your marriage. Put into effect what you have learned about the 6 Pillars of Intimacy.

This isn't a theory. This is your framework. This is your answer.

It's your turn to be like this couple:

We've been working on the pillars with intention for six full months now, and I am 100 percent sure it's given us a new perspective on just about every area of our marriage. We had EVERY intimacy challenge and EVERY communication challenge, and honestly, we thought, "It is what it is."

If you doubt things can change, they can. Have the

hard conversations and lean into the Lord, each other, and the guiding principles of the ONE Family. You'll be better for it, we promise!

— *L. I. (wife)*

WHO'S HOLDING YOU ACCOUNTABLE?

As you face this fork in the road—determining if this book will just be another marriage book or a resource for creating transformation—one question to ask is, "Who's holding you accountable to the changes you wish to see in your marriage?"

Some of you will say you and your spouse will be accountable to each other. This is an option, if the two of you can stay on the same team. However, in our many years studying marriage, we've seen so many couples struggle to be accountable to one another. If your spouse is the one holding you accountable for the changes, and you don't take action, he/she is unlikely to say anything. No one wants to feel like a parent or a nag or a complainer.

You might not have anyone who would keep you accountable. If that's you, know that you are 100 percent normal. Most couples don't have anyone in their world who is keeping them accountable to change. Most couples don't have marriage mentors. It's easier to think about getting help in your fitness or finances or careers or parenting...but marriage? Sometimes you can't even imagine having a coach.

As you stand at the fork in the road, who can you trust to hold you accountable? Who understands what you are trying to accomplish by understanding and embracing the 6 Pillars of Intimacy? Find people with whom you can be vulnerable and transparent. You don't have to start this journey of strengthening the 6 Pillars of Intimacy by yourself.

Throughout this book, you have been introduced to couples just like you. Couples who had a pillar or two or three that had cracks and realized they needed help to strengthen those pillars. These couples tried to change things on their own; they read books, listened to podcasts, and tried other things but were still stuck. Things changed for them when they started marriage coaching. Each of these couples got the strategy, structure, and accountability they needed to create their own extraordinary marriage. You can too! If you want to learn more about marriage coaching go to oneextraordinarymarriage.com/coaching.

It's not a weakness to be coached; in fact, the most successful people in any area get support to achieve their goals and dreams. If you are ready to take action around the 6 Pillars of Intimacy, it's time. Build a team around you—your spouse, your coach, your community—and let's take action together!

You're ready! And we are cheering you on!

It's time to put this framework into action. It is time to build an extraordinary marriage. You're ready to break the cycles that haven't been working and strengthen your pillars. We know what's possible, and we can't wait to see you achieve the extraordinary in your marriage using the 6 Pillars of Intimacy!

ACKNOWLEDGEMENTS

It is impossible to write a book of this magnitude without thanking God for not only the inspiration but the persistence to make this happen. If it wasn't for our relationship with our Heavenly Father and our awareness of his true design for marriage, The 6 Pillars of Intimacy would not exist.

Thank you ONE Family, for being extraordinary, for sharing your stories with us, for allowing us to be a part of your marriage — no matter what season you are in. You are the reason that we fight for marriages day in and day out. We love you guys!

To my coaching clients, it is an honor and a privilege to walk alongside you as you navigate the toughest seasons in your marriage. I do not take for granted the trust that you have placed in me.

We are forever grateful to Ps. Jurgen and Ps. Leanne for choosing to come to the United States in 2005 to start Awaken Church in San Diego. Your boldness has inspired us to take a stand for marriage and continue to fight even when others say give up.

Ps. Jon and Ps. Becky, thank you for showing us what

it means to operate with excellence. You have been our campus pastors since we first walked into Awaken in 2015 and have shaped how we do what we do. Your prayers and words of encouragement have never wavered.

Ps. Matt and Ps. Mikala, thank you for believing that couples need to invest in themselves. During a pandemic, you, along with the entire leadership team at Awaken Church, hosted a Marriage Reset for couples, and you invited us to speak. It was this invitation that allowed us to share the concept of The 6 Pillars of Intimacy for the very first time.

Thank you, Ritchie and Carolyn, for being the first ones to tell us to write this book. It was your encouragement that took The 6 Pillars of Intimacy from one 60 minute presentation to a blueprint for couples around the world.

To Scott and Alana, Chris and Cheryl, Andre and Shaunna, Mike and Angel, Jon and Theresa, Joel and Dana, and Ernie and Fiona, thank you for being our cheerleaders. You were never too busy to respond to a phone call or a text or even just sitting around the firepit talking about the dream for this book. You have been there through it all and have never wavered in your faith that this book would move mountains. Friends like you are rare, and we are beyond blessed to have each of you in our lives.

We are grateful to Self Publishing School and especially our coach, Kerk, for the wisdom and strategy to get this book done. We recognized we could not do this on our own and you were there every step of the way, pushing us forward, keeping us on track.

To our editing team at Wandering Words, thank you for the tough love that you showed in the editing process. Your questions and suggestions made this book so much more than it ever would have been if we had tried to do it ourselves. Working with you reminded us it's often better to bring in the experts when you are working on a project instead of trying to do it all by yourself.

To our children, thank you for understanding why we do what we do, even when it is embarrassing for you. You are the reason that we continue to fight for marriage. We want you and your peers to know that marriage is not a disposable relationship, that couples can work through tough times and that marriage can get better over time.

And finally, to our first marriage role models, our parents, thank you for demonstrating to us what a lifelong commitment means. We are grateful that you didn't hide the struggles and even more grateful that you worked through the challenges. Even in our darkest hours of marriage, divorce was off the table because of the example that you set.

DO YOU NEED PERSONAL HELP TO IMPROVE YOUR MARRIAGE?

Have you been struggling to create the extraordinary marriage you desire?

Does it seem like the two of you keep repeating the same arguments over and over again?

Do you need help implementing The 6 Pillars of Intimacy?

If you answered yes to any of these questions it's time to take action!

Apply for coaching today by visiting:
https://oneextraordinarymarriage.com/coaching

ABOUT THE AUTHORS

Tony and Alisa DiLorenzo are sought-after speakers, podcast hosts, and coaches on the topics of sex, love, and marriage. They share the hardships and triumphs they have had in their marriage through their site at ONE Extraordinary Marriage. Through their stories, energy, and passion, they inspire couples to live an extraordinary marriage.

Having dealt with the issues of pornography, financial crisis, and child loss, they understand the issues that impact relationships and trust. They work with couples around the world, equipping them with the tools and strategies they need to rebuild broken trust.

Tony and Alisa have been featured on FOX News, The CW, ESPN Radio, Lifestyle Magazine, Good Housekeeping, and MSN Living. They are the authors of several best selling books, including the 7 Days of Sex Challenge. Their podcast is consistently #1 in marriage on Apple Podcast, with an audience around the world.

LEAVE A REVIEW

Love this book? Don't forget to let others know.

Every review matters, and it matters a lot!

Head over to Amazon or wherever you purchased
The 6 Pillars of Intimacy: The Secret to an Extraordinary
Marriage to leave an honest review for us.

We're truly honored and blessed to have you part of the
ONE Family.

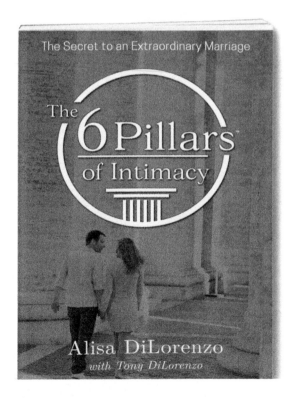

NOTES

Introduction

1. Dillow, Joseph, et. al. *Intimacy Ignited: Conversations Couple to Couple*. Colorado: Navpress, 2004

2. Gaspard, Terry. "Timing is Everything When It Comes to Marriage Counseling." *The Gottman Institute,* 23 July 2015. https://www.gottman.com/blog/timing-is-everything-when-it-comes-to-marriage-counseling/. Accessed 18 August 2021.

Chapter 1: What No One Ever Told You About Marriage

1. Follows, Stephen. "How Many People Work On a Movie?" *Stephen Follows Film Data and Education,* 6 April 2020. https://stephenfollows.com/how-many-people-work-on-a-movie/ Accessed 18 August 2021.

Chapter 3: Set Yourself Up For Success

1. MJJ Music. "Man In The Mirror" *Michael Jackson.* https://www.michaeljackson.com/track/man-mirror/ Accessed 4 September 2021

Chapter 6: Pillar #2 — Physical Intimacy

1. @oneextraordinarymarriage. (2020) When it comes to kissing your spouse are your kisses usually deep and sensual or a quick peck? Instagram story July 2020.

2. Penn Medicine. "Can You Kiss and Hug Your Way to Better Health? Research Says Yes." *Penn Medicine,* 8 January 2018. https://www.pennmedicine.org/updates/blogs/health-and-wellness/2018/february/affection Accessed 2 September 2021

3. Anderer, John. "Xs & Os: Couples Who Regularly Show Physical Affection Have Happier Relationships" *Study Finds,* 29 April 2020. https://www.studyfinds. org/couples-who-regularly-engage-in-physical-affection-have-happier-relationships/ Accessed 2 September 2021

Chapter 7: Pillar #3 — Financial Intimacy

1. Cruze, Rachel. "Money, Marriage and Communication: The Link Between Relationship Problems and Finances" *Ramsey Solutions,* 28 April 2021. https://www.ramseysolutions.com/relationships/money-marriage-communication-research Accessed 28 September 2021.

2. LegalZoom Staff. "Estate Planning Statistics" *LegalZoom,* 25 August 2021. https://www.legalzoom.com/articles/estate-planning-statistics Accessed 28 August 2021.

Chapter 8: Pillar #4 — Spiritual Intimacy

1. "Effects of Religious Practice on Marriage" *Marripedia.* http://marripedia.org/effects_of_religious_practice_on_marriage Accessed 22 August 2021.

Chapter 9: Pillar #5 — Recreational Intimacy

1. Heel That Pain. "8 Health Benefits of Having Fun" *Heel That Pain,* 14 March 2016. https://heelthatpain.com/8-health-benefits-of-having-fun/ Accessed 20 September 2021.

2. Crespo, Rebecca. "10 Simple Benefits of Having Fun" *Minimalism Made Simple,* 2020. https://www.minimalismmadesimple.com/home/having-fun/ Accessed 20 September 2021.

3. Smith, Sam Benson. "This Weekly Routine Is Statistically Proven to Save Your Relationship" *Reader's Digest,* 22 August 2017. https://www.rd.com/article/date-night-great-for-couples/ Accessed 17 August 2021.

4. Wilcox, W. Bradford and Jeffrey Dew. "The Date Night Opportunity: What Does Couple Time Tell Us About the Potential Value of Date Nights?" *National Marriage Project,* 2012. http://nationalmarriageproject.org/wp-content/uploads/2012/05/NMP-DateNight.pdf Accessed 22 August 2021.

5. Benson, Harry and Steve McKay. "'Date Nights' Strengthen Marriages" *Marriage Foundation,* September 2016. https://marriagefoundation.org.uk/wp-content/uploads/2016/09/MF-paper-Date-Nights-Sep-2016-1.pdf Accessed 22 August 2021.

Chapter 10: Pillar #6 — Sexual Intimacy

1. Wolfson, Elijah. "12 Ways Sex Helps You Live Longer" *Healthline,* 10 October 2019. https://www.healthline.com/health/ways-sex-helps-you-live-longer Accessed 23 August 2021.

2. Spitz, Aaron. *The Penis Book.* Emmaus: Rodale Inc., 2018.

3. Gunter, Jen. *The Vagina Bible.* New York: Citadel Press, 2019.

4. Feuerman, Marni. "Is Pornography Destroying Your Marriage?" Very Well Mind, 6 November 2020. https://www.verywellmind.com/is-pornography-destroying-your-marriage-2302509 Accessed 4 September 2021.

5. Brito, Janet. "Why You're Having Less Sex with Your Partner — and How to Get Back Into It" *Healthline,* 13 January 2020. https://www.healthline.com/health/healthy-sex/sexless-marriage Accessed 4 September 2021.

Printed in Great Britain
by Amazon

81504710R00114